RAW TALKS WITH WISDOM

MIKE PASCHALL

NOT YOUR GRANDMA'S DEVO

volume 1
JANUARY, FEBRUARY, MARCH

RAW TALKS WITH WISDOM - Not Your Grandma's Devo
Volume 1 - (January, February, & March).

Copyright © 2013, 2018 by Michael D. Paschall.

All rights reserved. No part of this book may be reproduced or stored in a retrieval system, or transmitted in any form or by any means—electronic, mechanical, photocopying, recording, or otherwise, without the written permission of owner.

FIRST EDITION

ISBN: 978-0-578-41057-9

Cover & Title Page: Jon C. Egan

CONTENTS

Preface   v

Dedication   ix

JANUARY   1 - 49

FEBRUARY   53 - 102

MARCH   105 - 157

Endnotes   159

Resources & Other Helps   161

Acknowledgements   165

Author   169

PREFACE

HEY! Thank you so much for giving *RAW TALKS WITH WISDOM – Not Your Grandma's Devo* a whirl! It's an honor and a blessing to have you along for the ride. Before we get started, I thought it would be helpful to give you an idea of what this thing is all about.

FOUNDATIONS

Setting aside time every day for a devotional is probably one of the best disciplines I was ever encouraged to implement into my daily life. It has provided me countless connections with the Lord.

For the past 35 years, I have primarily read devotionals by two men, Dr. James Sidlow Baxter and Oswald Chambers. I was introduced to Dr. Baxter in 1978 by my first real spiritual mentor: Dr. H. D. McCarty. I heard Brother Sidlow speak on more than one occasion. He was already in his late '70s by the time I was introduced to his written work. I will always be thankful for **AWAKE MY HEART**. I learned so much from the meditations in that devotional.

Our friends, Earl and Barbara Patrick, gave me my first copy of **MY UTMOST FOR HIS HIGHEST** by Oswald Chambers when I was ordained in April 1986. I still use that same copy. I can't begin to describe the blessing that devotional has been to me. Chambers' revelations are amazing, especially considering he was only 43 years old when he died in 1917. His wife, Biddy, compiled transcripts and notes that eventually evolved into **UTMOST**, first published in 1927. I am forever in debt to them both for what was spoken, captured, and put into print for all of us to benefit.

MY DESIRE

My prayer is that the Lord will speak to you through *RAW TALKS WITH WISDOM – Not Your Grandma's Devo*. I have always gained wisdom and perspective by reading scripture and devotionals, but more important to me has been how the Holy Spirit tailors each lesson to fit my life. It doesn't really mean anything unless we can practically apply truth to the joys and tears of the now.

If all you come away with after working through these devotionals is more knowledge, then I'd have to really evaluate if it was all worth it. I would encourage you to take it to another level, beyond mere theology and theory, into the realms of practical reality—stuff you can wear, taste, and feel. I want you to know He gave you revelation!

MY VISION

It's simple. Do this devotional the way you would do any other devotional. But what I really want is for these daily lessons to stimulate journaling (which is the reason for the **"In the Pages"** questions at the end of each day). I would encourage you to make an appointment to meet with the Lord each day, and then stick with it. Daily appointments can become healthy habits in a relatively short period of time. Pick a time each day that "works" best for you, and make Him a priority!

I want the material to stick with you. I want you to chew on it throughout your day. I want you to discuss it over coffee with a friend or colleague. Stuff like that. My ultimate prayer is that ***RAW TALKS WITH WISDOM – Not Your Grandma's Devo*** adds value to your quiet times with the Lord!

Like I said, I want you to do this devotional the way you do devotionals. But here is the method I would use to tackle each day:

First, read the **entire chapter** of Proverbs for that day. If the day is June 11, then read all of Proverbs chapter 11.

Then read the focus verses that begin each devo.

Third, read the devotional itself.

Fourth, journal your responses to the **In The Pages** questions at the end, along with anything else you feel compelled to write about. Get yourself a good leather-bound journal! Your thoughts and prayers deserve a proper container.

Lastly, spend some time in prayer and meditation.

That is the vision.

I sincerely hope the Holy Spirit will speak to you through these devotionals and give you things to write about in your journal. I also hope these devotionals will get you in the habit of reading through all of Proverbs twelve times in one year. For as long as I have been soaking in Proverbs, I have found a surprise almost every time! A new perspective, a nugget of value, something I've never seen before. It has to be the Holy Spirit that does that, and so far, I love the process!

WHY *RAW TALKS WITH WISDOM – Not Your Grandma's Devo*?

It dawned on me one day that our relationships with the Lord should always be raw. I was stuck in the rut of religious activity for far too long! What I have with Him now feels very real, relaxed, and extremely relevant.

I live and work in a culture that is filled with young and old ideas. I have definitely mellowed over the years and learned how to slow down. I think this season is teaching me to be more focused on the stuff that actually counts. To say it, whatever "it" really is, without apology and with serious conviction.

I'm not a theologian. I know that. So there is no use in my trying to be one. I'm a weird mixture of stuff with a rich experience of failure and profound grace. **RAW TALKS WITH WISDOM** – *Not Your Grandma's Devo* is a title that feels like me. It gives me permission to be myself and say things like I really do.

I know the angels won't sing along to every single one of these devotionals for you. But maybe, just maybe, some of it will help someone, somewhere, turn and embrace the **RAW** truth of God's wisdom.

Michael D. Paschall
2013

For those who follow.

The Journey Begins

January 1
Proverbs 1

"These are the wise sayings of Solomon, David's son, Israel's king - written down so we'll know how to live well and right, to understand what life means and where it's going; a manual for living, for learning what's right and just and fair; to teach the inexperienced the ropes and give our young people a grasp on reality. There's something here also for seasoned men and women, still a thing or two for the experienced to learn – fresh wisdom to probe and penetrate, the rhymes and reasons of wise men and women." Proverbs 1:1-6, MSG

Happy New Year! I hope you feel as good today as you did before you went out last night! -*smile*-

Another promise of 365 days peers over the surface of the earth. Each of us is to venture into the unknown mystery that we call time. It seems now, more than ever before, we desperately need the voice of sound wisdom and wise judgment about how to conduct all the affairs of our "techno-colored" lives.

Humanity has advanced in so many ways, improving the ease and quality of life for the masses, but it seems we continue to cycle in vacuums of unhealthy paradigms and cultures of living that do not always put forth the highest and best for each other's consideration.

Prejudice in all forms still lives, families struggle, marriage is no longer valued like it once was, divorce is too common, we do not trust our government, we do not trust our religious leaders, people are addicted to whatever kills their pain, our kids are easily swept up in the currents of trends and image, and there is way too much debris from our "falling short" (Romans 3:23).

Exploits of kindness and true concern do happen, but we are more surprised when they *do* happen than when they do not. The truth is, we need help! "S#%t" happens (*By the way, this will be the first and last time in this devotional that I will censor the language. From here on out, I will say what I'm thinking – fair warning*), and we need the prudent, saturated wisdom from heaven. We need another perspective that brings light and clarity in a world that seems to settle too much in the dark hue of gray.

It will not hurt for us to brush up on our manners and protocols relating to how we treat our brothers and sisters who share space on our blessed orb.

I am predisposed to the idea that GOD LOVES US and really does have viable suggestions which point to a better way than the ways we tend to choose on our own. And we DO get to choose. Wisdom jumps and yells from *Proverbs*, *"Pick me! Pick me! Ooh-ooh, pick me!"* Then we make our choice.

My grandmother used to say,

> ***"Sometimes a person just has to climb fools' hill!"***

We have all done it. But we do not want to make that a regular occurrence. So we need to pack as much help and truth as possible into our grids so that when those moments of temptation and opportunity present themselves, hopefully we will allow the smooth and peaceful words of disciplined wisdom to rule the way we respond. I need that this next year. We need that.

Let's choose to make the journey with Lady Wisdom at our side!

In The Pages

Read Proverbs 14:12-14. Write a paraphrase of that verse's significance. What do you already see in front of you for this next year that requires the voice of Wisdom for settled direction and peace in your life?

God's Desire

January 2
Proverbs 2

"For the LORD gives wisdom; from HIS mouth come knowledge and understanding." Proverbs 2:6, NASB

"But if any of you lacks wisdom, let him ask of God, who gives to all generously and without reproach, and it will be given him." James 1:5, NASB

In the Old Testament we read a story about a dream that young King Solomon had. In this dream, God tells Solomon, *"Ask what you wish me to give you"* (1 Kings 3:5, NASB). The dialogue between Solomon and God is simply magnificent! Solomon had witnessed God do so many good things during his father's reign as king that he had confidence God could do the same for him.

He quickly acknowledged his need for divine help and guidance. He also humbled himself and admitted that he was way in over his head and that the task of being king was much too big for his own natural gifts and abilities.

Then, Solomon knocks it out of the park!

"Here's what I want: Give me a God-listening heart so I can lead your people well, discerning the difference between good and evil. For who on their own is capable of leading your glorious people" (1 Kings 3:9, MSG*)*.

Next, he awakens, realizes it was a dream and that God was talking to him, goes to Jerusalem to sacrifice in the presence of God, and then throws a huge party for all of his servants! This is crazy good!

I get excited about this because God was revealing His own desire for what he yearned from Solomon. The new king was "tuned in" enough to hear God's heart and sensitive enough to go with the flow that God wanted. God baited Solomon, primed the pump for success, and the boy flat-out took the bait and ran with it.

I do not believe for one second that God's desire for you and for me is any less! James points out in today's focus verse that God is willing to give wisdom to anyone and everyone who asks him for it. What a fabulous promise! We need wisdom, we need discernment, and we need knowledge from Him. God wants to cooperate and help us as we live out our lives.

If He were interested in controlling us, He would not have given us our own will and opportunities to choose what we do. He has simply offered His help and given insight. It is actually a little overwhelming if you really think about it: **God as counselor and friend**. But, the possibility is ever before us.

 If there was ever a time that we needed His help... it is now!

In The Pages

Describe what is on your short list if God asked you, "What do you want?" What current events in your life demand wisdom from above?

Belly Punch

January 3
Proverbs 3

"Blessed are those who find wisdom, those who gain understanding, for she is more profitable than silver and yields better returns than gold. She is more precious than rubies; nothing you desire can compare with her." Proverbs 3:13-15, NIV

Wisdom tells us that we can be happy in this world when we are tapped into the kind of truth that defines the real value of life. In other words, material "things" cannot compare to the value of God's insight and direction. By looking around in our western culture, many might disagree with that thought. But having more things, more toys, more *stuff* doesn't necessarily equate to happiness, fulfillment, and joy.

To the contrary, having more things, along with the labor required to maintain those comforts, can actually be the source of great frustration and pain in life. Today's text confirms that hypothesis.

Jesus had a tender way of asking disturbing questions. Those questions could either keep you awake at night or just flat out punch you in the belly.

He once asked his disciples, *"For what will it profit a man if he gains the whole world and forfeits his soul" (*Matthew 16:26, NASB*)*. To *"forfeit"* speaks of *"damage,"* or *"to suffer loss,"* but not necessarily to terminate. The entire context is about us living our lives as servants to God's purpose.

Decisions towards that purpose cost us the luxury and freedom of just doing what we want all the time. There is another agenda, another pace or another purpose in how we value our priorities.

A decision to live in the ebb and flow of God's rhythm suggests that we seek the Lord's perspectives about what we give ourselves to. That is what Wisdom is declaring and confirming. Happiness awaits us when we have clarity and a submissive heart towards His suggestions and insight for our lives.

Yes, ultimately we get to decide. But He is more than willing to point us in the right direction. Maybe some of our *stuff* gets in the way of this process. Maybe circumstance has us reacting out of our emotions or fears. The invitation is to seek Wisdom and understanding from a position that knows all and sees all. It can be precious to us!

In The Pages

Describe the last time you made a quick decision that might have better served if you would have had clearer guidance from Wisdom. Explain your process when trying to hear from the Holy Spirit about your concerns and needs for direction.

Dad Stuff

January 4
Proverbs 4

"Hear, O sons, the instruction of a father, and give attention that you may gain understanding," Proverbs 4:1, NASB

The Hebrew word for *"instruction"* is **mûçâr** (pronounced *moo-sawr'*). It means, *"discipline, chastening or correction."* Usually, those words bring an uncomfortable feeling to our heart. Guess it would depend on the kind of "instruction" you got when you were a kid. Growing up, I received plenty of "talks," deserved groundings, and I also got my butt spanked when all other options were not working.

I was stubborn and a slow learner. Oh, I was plenty smart, but I always had my own ideas about what I wanted to do. My dad and mom had tender spirits, so I knew that they would spank only as a last resort.

I have a buddy who grew up with a belt constantly draped over the door handle to his room. Not only were there real threats, but easy access to whippings that happened on an almost daily basis. Needless to say, my friend had a really hard time using physical discipline with his own children. His grown kids are brilliant, model citizens, so whatever method he used worked just fine.

The bottom line here is that the father, parent, whoever, uses whatever method is necessary to convey help and understanding. I didn't ever see the wisdom and genius of the wise counsel of my father until I was about 18 years old. I always just thought my parents took stupid pills and that they would figure it out one day.

It so happened that I was a freshman in college and was clueless about what I wanted to do with my life. I was totally unstable and unable to land anywhere in peace. One weekend, I had my first real encounter with alcohol. Southern Comfort might be its name, but it took me on a trip to the pain zone. I was hung over for two days! I did all the things that a sick person does and more. I could not get out of bed because of the freight train that was clickity-clacking in my head. It was horrible.

Those two days, my parents did not say a word to me. They took care of me, but nothing was ever mentioned. A couple days later, Dad invited me to his office. He wanted to talk to me in private. I was in great dread of that meeting!

To my surprise, he shared some things with me out of his childhood along with a few of the lessons he had learned around his own mistakes with alcohol. Things I never knew, stories I never imagined. I still recall what he wore that day, I remember how he smelled and I was deeply impacted by the fact that he did not demean me, but instead challenged me to responsibility.

I honestly believe that the "way" he handled the discipline made the difference. Not once, since that sloppy weekend, have I ever been out of control with alcohol. Not because I abstain, but because my father's graceful and wise counsel worked. I understood... and that is the point!

Thanks Dad! xo

In The Pages

How did your parents respond to your worst mistake? How did it affect you? If it was handled badly, have you forgiven them? What does discipline with purpose look like? What does discipline just out of emotion result in?

Rattlesnakes

January 5
Proverbs 5

"Dear friend, pay close attention to this, my wisdom; listen very closely to the way I see it. Then you'll acquire a taste for good sense; what I tell you will keep you out of trouble." Proverbs 5:1-2, MSG

I've always studied, preached and taught out of the New American Standard Ryrie Study Bible. It was the first bible given to me by my bride after I gave my life to the Lord while in college. Dr. Ryrie breaks down the topics of Proverbs into 24 major segments. I am sure it is not an all-inclusive list, but those 24 categories are predominately the focus points of Wisdom's teaching.

One of the most common "Big Kahuna" warnings of Proverbs swirls around the havoc of adultery. We are not required to be astrophysicists to understand the life-ache that adultery poses. You want to talk about trouble? It is off the charts complicated and life changing.

To have your marriage touched by adultery or to touch someone else's marriage via a little "hanky-panky" is asking for big time, heart-wrecking, family-splitting trouble. That is not to say that supernatural grace cannot bring healing and recovery, but there is nothing sensible or right in adultery.

**It makes more sense to fill your bed with rattlesnakes
than to fool around with the marriage covenant.**

We will hit this topic often and hard throughout this devotional series. Too much is at stake to ignore the discussion.

"For when you were slaves of sin, you were free in regard to righteousness. Therefore, what benefits were you then deriving from the things of which you are now ashamed? For the outcome of those things is death" (Romans 6:20-21, NASB).

In other words, when you were unaware of God's love for you, it would not be all that strange that you had a sinner's lifestyle. Sin *is* the natural by-product of people who do not know how much God loves them. That is why Christians are not to be judgmental of people who spiritually do not know any better than to continue in sin. Our job is to live a better way before them—not to judge them.

But once we know better, once we have had an internal heart change concerning our identity, those old ways continuing in our lives only make us feel and act out of sorts with our new identity. There is a stench of death on the stuff that is contrary to *"Christ in me the hope of glory!"*

Our appreciation of the wisdom of Proverbs should be on the increase by now. We need to listen closely. We ought to tap into the truth that can help steer us and keep us on the paths of peace and freedom. It is a better way to live.

In The Pages

What is the difference in noticing the debris in a person's life due to bad life choices versus flat out judging them?

Surety

January 6
Proverbs 6

"My son, if you become surety for your friend, if you have shaken hands in pledge for a stranger, you are snared by the words of your mouth; you are taken

by the words of your mouth. So do this, my son, and deliver yourself; for you have come into the hand of your friend: go and humble yourself; plead with your friend. Give no sleep to your eyes, nor slumber to your eyelids. Deliver yourself like a gazelle from the hand of the hunter, and like a bird from the hand of the fowler." Proverbs 6:1-5, NKJV

My wife and I have never been the kind of people anyone would mistake for having money. We have always ministered to small congregations, driven used cars, and mostly rented wherever we lived. No complaints here! We have never missed a meal and HE has faithfully met our needs.

But it has always been obvious that we do not run with the rich and famous. All of that to say, we rarely have been asked by anyone to *"become surety"* for any kind of need. People have borrowed money from us, but it has only happened a couple of times.

Unfortunately, those few occasions stirred enough anxiety and agitation inside of me to drive home this truth of Wisdom in today's focus verses.

The real problem to our spirit is the fact that a friend or a family member might be involved. It looks "all good" on the front side. We are motivated by our emotions and loving desire to help; no one wants to withhold from someone they love and care about. So we cave in, write the check, dig in the cookie jar, cash in the CD, make the loan or co-sign on the note.

It is all grins as long as everything goes according to plan.

But since when does everything ever go according to plan? I figure that Patti and I are about 50-50 in recovering what we have loaned. And those times we lost money were definitely bothersome! The arguments and discussions in my mind usually became vile and poisonous.

The judgments and the bitter thoughts actually made us sick to the point that the only relief was to absolutely "forgive" the debt and release the one who owed us the money.

One of the largest risks that Patti and I ever ventured was personally financing, in a "second" position, the selling of our home. Not a penny of that was ever recovered when the buyer's negligence prompted foreclosure proceedings. The topic seldom surfaces, but when it does, we usually just call each other "stupid" and have a good laugh.

For the most part, we are done with being surety. We will "give" when we can, and as He leads, but making a business arrangement with our friends or family is not what's best for our hearts. If someone wants to "pay it back," that will be fine, but we will have already resolved that it is a gift and expect no return.

It is the only way we will sleep sound at night. As old as these Proverbs are, they are still very current and relevant in truth, aren't they?

In The Pages

What are your thoughts about Wisdom's lesson today? Have you been a victim or the "cause" in a loan gone wrong? Are you at peace with it? Is there more that you need to do to square the deal?

Good Water - Bad Water

January 7
Proverbs 7

"Talk to Wisdom as to a sister. Treat Insight as your companion. They'll be with you to fend off the Temptress—that smooth-talking, honey-tongued Seductress." Proverbs 7:4-5, MSG

"But He answered and said to the one who told Him, 'Who is My mother and who are My brothers?' And He stretched out His hand toward His disciples and said, 'Here are My mother and My brothers! For whoever does the will of My Father in heaven is My brother and sister and mother'." Matthew 12:48-50, NKJV

I am fond of the personification of Wisdom and also the negative expressions of those things that we end up living with if we are not careful. I am visual, so it helps me see. I've added the Matthew passage to today's text because Jesus often used the same concept to get his major points across.

It's truly beautiful to think that we are family, close family, when we pursue God's desire for our lives. It is like Jesus is saying, *"Beloved, thanks for asking. Come on in, let me get you a cup of coffee, let's sit and talk about it!"* It helps me to see these kinds of things.

So we are invited to converse with Lady Wisdom, to hold her, love her, and treat her as a faithful sister whom we can share anything with. We are also encouraged to seek Wisdom's insight into our lives. Combined, they help us fend off the Temptress who Peterson describes as the *"smooth-talking, honey-tongued Seductress."*

The NASB calls her the *"adulterer."* Although we recognize the perils of such a thing, I think our religious bent sometimes gives us tunnel vision. We think as long as we are not "sleeping around" that we are safe from the Seductress.

Honestly, when it comes to fooling around, I think we have many more temptations to face than just sexual impropriety and unfaithfulness. Think for a moment about the things in your life that oppose your desire to live for Christ or challenge your commitment to responsibility.

**An "affair" could be with just about anything.
It doesn't have to be with a person!**

We get tired and empty and it is very easy for us to start looking for the fastest and easiest way to "fill up" again. This is where our challenge awaits. Which well will we drink from?

We need water, living-water, but we seem to find alternative wells that are not good for us. We see, we desire, we taste, we sip, and then we drink deeply from a false source that will eventually lay claim on our heart.

Without it ever being the initial desire, we realize that we have invited the mistress or the seducer to occupy ground in our lives that should not be there.

Things that should be priority become secondary, and things that should be secondary, become priority. This is not the *"abundant life"* He promised us! If we do not pay attention to these details, our life can get jacked-up in a heartbeat!

I am a freedom guy! With kilt lifted, let us scream over ourselves, "FREEDOM!" Not everything that I am free to do is good for me. I have discovered that the water HE has for me satisfies my every need and deepest desires. The same is true for you too.

In The Pages

We know what seduces us. How much ground have you given "it" lately? We need a balance of external protection and internal truth to fend off being blindsighted. How are your security measures with your biggest challenges?

Hollering

January 8
Proverbs 8

"Does not wisdom call, and understanding lift up her voice? On top of the heights beside the way, where the paths meet, she takes her stand." Proverbs 8:1-2, NASB

"Listen as Wisdom calls out! Hear as understanding raises her voice! On the hilltop along the road, she takes her stand at the crossroads." Proverbs 8:1-2, NLT

As a child, and on into my college years, I had a best friend. We were inseparable. His home was my home, my home was his home; everything was shared—the good, the bad, and sometimes, the ugly.

Early on, our parents lived across the street from one another. So being with each other only required crossing a sleepy narrow street. Separation from my buddy usually occurred only at meal times.

His mama had a powerful voice with octaves that swayed branches! Even from my backyard or most anywhere in the neighborhood, we could easily hear,

"Bobbyyyyyyyyyyy!"

That meant: heads up, pay attention, everything stops, time to go! I can still hear that singsong beacon alerting my friend that it was time to run home.

These days, we want our homes airtight and soundproof. We do not want any outside interference to interrupt the quality of our fancy home entertainment systems. Noise outside is not welcome inside.

Kids seldom play in the yard anymore either. It's not okay for kids to explore on their bicycles. It is too sketchy. We do not know our neighbors. It is rare for us to walk onto another person's property.

We email and text, but we do not talk over the fence like we used to do. We grab the remote, crank up the sound, and drown out the big bad outside.

Today's text pictures Lady Wisdom in the streets of our lives, calling out, yelling requests and instructions like Bobby's mom:

***"Heed my voice, pay attention, listen to me—
choose the lucidity of Godly wisdom!"***

It is not uncommon in third world countries to hear all kinds of advertising and solicitations from venders selling and hawking their wares via bullhorns and loud speakers in the streets. But for us, we need another avenue. With all the commotion around us, we need the voice of the Holy Spirit to help us sort through life. It is hectic out there.

We are too busy, over committed, not really rested, and lacking opportunities to settle into internal solitude. This is why it's so important for us to set aside time in our days to hear from the Lord, to meditate on His word, and to avail our ears to the voice of Wisdom.

She is calling your name. It's time to run back home. Dinner is served.

In The Pages

How does it affect your day when you feel certain you have connected with the Lord in your quiet time? See John 14:15-17, 16:13. Is your confidence stirred by these promises? How so?

He Knows

January 9
Proverbs 9

"The fear of the Lord is the beginning of wisdom, and the knowledge of the Holy One is understanding." Proverbs 9:10, NASB

This is pretty much the entire theme of Proverbs. We hear it for the first time in *Proverbs 1:7*. Wisdom is a deep water that covers a multitude of ideas and concepts. Today's verse highlights the initial realization that our submission to the heart of God is the "inception" of our hand-in-hand stroll down life's path with Wisdom.

We know that *"the fear of the Lord"* is not an unhealthy trepidation of trying to satisfy an angry God. It is more like a fit understanding that God is for us, loves us, wants us, and desires our happiness and blessings. It sounds a little candy-coated, but it is truth.

And notice that I did not put "comfort" on that list. One of my best friends often says, *"God is much more interested in our character development than our comfort."*[1] We forget that.

Too many people have a horrible image of God the Father. If your Dad beat the crap out of you, divorced your mom for the hot chick at the office, or abandoned the family when you were a kid, it is very understandable that you might see God as angry, distant, and always looking to bust your chops.

Maybe your mother suffered rejection as a child or young woman, and as a result, she was disconnected to her nurture instincts in raising you. That would probably affect your ability to see God as someone who really cares about your pain or need for comfort and security.

How we were raised *does* mess with our views of God!

Go check out Hebrews 4:16. The *"therefore"* points to the precluding discussion in the text, that Jesus understands our humanity and the fact that we "blow it" in our lives at times. He knows our sin dilemmas and internal weaknesses; He experienced temptations that we so often face.

So we still have our issues down here, but God sees it all, and He still loves us deeply. Believe it or not, He is not plotting our next butt whipping. That is the richness of Proverbs. God is willing to partner with us, and to help us traverse some of our rocky streams.

Developing our relationships with God is about the smartest thing we ever do. Not everyone has eyes to see this, but I believe it with all of my heart.

At the time of this writing, our daughter's twins just had their 2nd birthday. The Elmo party was a huge success. They tore into each present and then immediately cast it aside in order to move onto the next package. They are 2 years old. What else would you expect?

They didn't have a single thought about what it cost us in time or cash to present them with those gifts. It was fun to see them enjoy their presents, but when they move towards Ba and Nana with uplifted arms, wanting to be picked up, the world stops turning! I sense it works like that with God.

Our moving towards Him in love and a real desire for intimacy is *His* real joy. He gives the wisdom for our growth and blessings. But our pursuit of Him... well, that IS the *"beginning"* of all wisdom.

In The Pages

How do you feel about your connection with the Lord right now? How are you predominately hearing Him? If you were responsible for helping another person develop his or her relationship with God, what would you suggest?

Hedging Truth

January 10
Proverbs 10

"The tongue of the righteous is as choice silver. The heart of the wicked is worth little." Proverbs 10:20, NASB

"A word out of your mouth may seem of no account, but it can accomplish nearly anything—or destroy it! It only takes a spark, remember, to set off a forest fire. A careless or wrongfully placed word out of your mouth can do that. By our speech we can ruin the world, turn harmony to chaos, throw mud on a reputation, send the whole world up in smoke and go up in smoke with it, smoke right from the pit of hell." James 3:5-6, MSG

"Choice silver": something to bank on, something to value, an instrument of true and trusted substance. The ability to trust a man or a woman by his or her words is an amazing and refreshing concept. Our culture thrives in the ability to "spin" and dazzle with words, but it rarely offers the real truth or precise information.

Turn on the evening news or surf over to watch any of the talking heads and see if you reel with more questions than answers?

My spiritual tribe talks of honor constantly. Integrity at every level is emphasized and expected. I have hung around in institutional church and ministry culture too long to be bamboozled by any romantic notion that Christians always tell the truth.

As long as **rejection** lives in the Body like a virus, people will always find it difficult to tell a story as it really happened. Even the most noble, respected, and anointed people struggle with keeping our facts and information solidly truthful. Again, it hurts us all for this kind of behavior to exist around us.

An exaggeration is not the truth. We used to call it a lie. But that is an ugly notion, and we typically take liberties that get us outside of the bounds that qualify as refinement of "choice silver."

This may be unnerving, but it is also not ok to fake or pretend around our ministry times at the church house. Too much that we see on religious television is not real; everything from the images of wealth and prosperity portrayed on a set, to the theatrics of personal ministry and showcasing of miracles and healings that do not really happen. This is shameful and totally unnecessary.

**God does not need us to "Hollywood" what He can
and will do at HIS discretion.**

It wrecks faith for all of us. It soils the trust of non-believers who sometimes risk and hope for something more than this shoddy kind of religious crap. I do not think this is okay with Wisdom. It is not okay with God. And it sure as hell shouldn't be okay with us!

In The Pages

Have you ever caught someone in a "white-lie?" What happened in your head and heart afterwards? What about you? Is this a struggle for you? Do you care too much about what people think that you sometimes fudge the truth? What practical lesson is taught in John 8:31-32?

It Matters

January 11
Proverbs 11

"A false balance is an abomination to the Lord, but a just weight is His delight."
Proverbs 11:1 NASB

That word *"abomination"* is a potent word. It's filled with all kinds of imagery of God's wrath, anger and dissatisfaction with a particular situation. Depending on which translation of the Bible you read, we only see the word a couple times in the New Testament.

Most references to *"abomination"* can be found in the Old Testament. The basic translation of the Hebrew and Greek wording conveys the simple message that God actually hates what is going on. It may just be me, but that kind of makes me nervous.

The picture here portrays ugly remnants of cheating in the market place. Although this issue is addressed many times in the Proverbs, here it is specifically attached to that sketchy word we have already mentioned.

Fortunately, we have laws in this country that protect the rights of consumers from false advertising, usury and fraud. But this seems to be tapping into something deeper.

It is the deception and taking unfair advantage of our God-given opportunities and another person's trust that ruffles His feathers so violently. The shearing of His unaware sheep *(and we are ALL His sheep)* does not sit so well with His Majesty.

Apparently, the Lord doesn't seem to have much of a problem with a business or any person making a fair profit in a legit line of work.

I used to be in the insurance business and it is the favorite pastime of our culture to complain about insurance premiums and the profits that insurance companies make. But those profits are vital to the fidelity of the promise made to the consumer through the insurance contract.

In other words, those profits and cash reserves are necessary to pay all claims in the event of any loss by the policyholder. If there are no profits, there are no monies to pay my claim!

So it is to my benefit that my insurance companies make a profit. Only then can I trust the contract and the solvency of the company I do business with.

Normally, we just want the cheapest deal, but there is more at risk than what we usually consider.

We need discernment. We need to be satisfied and secure about whom we do business with. Those who desire the blessing of God on their business need to take serious inventory about how they treat customers.

It matters that pricing and value are fair and just to those who buy our product. The Lord takes note of these things.

In The Pages

Read Matthew 21:12-13. What images are stirred in you about the Lord's heart towards cheating or robbery in the market place? What do you think was going on in the mind of the common man who watched and heard Jesus' explosion? What adjustments need to be made for you to be at peace in your own business or with whom you do business with? Are you confident that there is integrity at every level?

Crowns

January 12
Proverbs 12

"An excellent wife is the crown of her husband, but she who shames him is like rottenness in his bones." Proverbs 12:4, NASB

"A hearty wife invigorates her husband, but a frigid woman is cancer in the bones." Proverbs 12:4, MSG

I am attracted to Peterson's translation because it points to this kind of *"excellent wife"* as being a woman of passion, honesty and transparency—one who can give herself *fully* to her husband. This is electrifying in its concept! The fact that the husband recognizes these qualities in his wife brings him amazing honor and gratitude in his life.

Patti and I were taught long ago to refer to each other as royalty. She is my "queen" and I am her "king." Not that it gets weird, but these are gentle reminders to us that we are humbled servants to each other.

Too often, Ephesians 5:22 ends up being the entire message for a good Christian marriage: *"Wives, be subject to your own husbands, as to the Lord"* (NASB). But we actually need to begin reading with verse 18 in order to reach our full potential: *"...but be filled with the Holy Spirit"* (NASB).

Please take a moment and focus on verse 21: *"and be subject to one another in the fear of Christ"* (NASB).

The word for *"subject"* means *"to place yourself under the authority of another."* In other words, both the man AND the woman are to proactively submit themselves as servants to *"one another"* in such a way that actually stimulates their passion and desire for their mate's honor!

If only one person makes decisions in a relationship, then it's not much of a partnership, is it?

Today's verses focus on the wife. But in order for her to fulfill these verses from her core, she has to know her value... that her man unconditionally loves her!

It always requires the efforts of two people to make a marriage pop with this kind of chemistry. When it is working right, the angels sing! Most marital issues could easily be resolved with a little more communication and intentional service soaked in sincere humility. It does reap great rewards and eternal satisfaction!

In The Pages

Sir, take some time to journal the qualities of your wife. (If you're single, what do you think you're looking for in a woman?) What kind of thanks needs to be offered to Him for such a gift? Make time to tell her about these qualities you recognize!

Madame, if you are a crown, and the jewels on that crown are the attributes of your servitude, what does that crown look like? How does your husband serve you? Does he know you are grateful? (If you are single, what do you think you're looking for in a man?)

Ripples

January 13
Proverbs 13

"Adversity pursues sinners, but the righteous will be rewarded with prosperity." Proverbs 13:21, NASB

This verse puts me on edge a bit. We can be too assumptive in the inventory of our lives. I don't want to be guilty of default thinking. Being blessed with good things in my life doesn't necessarily mean that I'm righteous. Having hard things in your life does not automatically mean that you are a sinner.

I've spent too many hours asking God to show me my sin because of some "hard" circumstance I was going through. Most people who have issues with the Church or "church folk" have had unpleasant dealings with these kinds of ideas. I do not think this is what wisdom is implying in this verse!

I'm willing to repent for my sin, but I'm not willing to allow that to be my identity.

I am a son, yet I know I fall short often.

It may not always be visible to everyone around me, but there is stuff going on in my head and heart that I know is not in my best welfare. If and when these thoughts are released and become relatively active, they create a negative ripple. Whether the wave remains a ripple or becomes a tsunami, people are affected.

There is nothing more painful than facing the effects of my sin. Especially when I see the aftermath of that adversity on people I love and care about.

There is something very hopeful in the promise of wisdom that people, who pursue the Lord and are infected with His love, His grace, and His peace, receive good things from that kind of lifestyle. The concept of "sowing and reaping" is valid kingdom theology.

We can be confused into believing that a kingdom deposit should equal a natural withdrawal of money, riches and wealth. Kingdom prosperity does not always equate to more finances. It could be that our prosperity is tied to the presence of the Lord in our lives for happiness, health, favor, and the fulfillment of desire that genuinely brings us peace and contentment with what we have.

"Rewarded" (whatever that may be) is the promise! *"For You make him most blessed forever; You make him joyful with gladness in Your presence"* (Psalm 21:6, NASB). That's the wave we all want to ride!

In The Pages

Is there a hard thing that you are going through right now? What is your thinking about "why" this thing is happening? What are your thoughts about the "rewards" of righteousness? Write out a prayer of thanksgiving for the Lord's blessings in your life.

Magnanimous

January 14
Proverbs 14

"He who oppresses the poor taunts his Maker but he who is gracious to the needy honors Him." Proverbs 14:31, NASB

You do not have to hang out in Proverbs long before it is quite evident that God has a thing for the poor. And the rest of us are strongly warned about taking advantage of the privileges of our wealth without some consideration for those less fortunate.

Making a profit is not the problem!

Usury is the problem.

We cannot exploit our opportunities as if we have no regard for His watching. We have MORE responsibility to steward our dealings with the powerless, not less.

It is so important to tap into this concept because Wisdom points out that if we are not mindful, we can actually insult or disrespect the heart of God.

The graceful flow of humanity towards the poor, the broken and the less fortunate, delights the Lord. We tend to think of "poor" in terms of wealth or money, but look around: people are hurting and need some love. They need a kind word. They need a smile of hope and respect.

That cashier, who checked you out yesterday at *Lots of Cheap Crap*, the one with the bad hair dye, frumpy clothes, and the crabby attitude, needed grace more than she needed your snarky pushback. Wonder what her story is about?

She has a story. Could it be that whatever mountains she faces everyday have worn down her spirit? Do you think she is tired, weary, and might be sluggin' through as best as she can?

Whatever it is, can we agree that what you saw is not her whole story?

Knowing only in part can be a temptation to judgment and critical thoughts. He knows the truth—the whole truth. He is the only one who does. And there is something so redemptive in our gracious touch that honors Him. The world is starved for this kind of counter-flow!

In The Pages

So how did you do at the checkout line? What was your reaction to a sour experience? What would a *graceful* response do for them? For you? What goes on in your head and heart when you see the guy with the cardboard sign that reads, *"Hungry, will work for food"* at that busy street corner?

Stud Chick

January 15
Proverbs 15

"A gentle answer turns away wrath, but a harsh word stirs up anger." Proverbs 15:1, NIV

It seems that every time I face a situation where emotions and offended passions get escalated, and if I have some time to pray and consider what my verbal response should be, the Lord moves me towards much softer words than what I am actively formulating in my mind. Without fail, He helps me with this, especially in circumstances where I might be bringing correction or instruction to another person I am counseling.

My wife is quick to remind me that a "bad tone" can twist the way a message is heard. If she doesn't like the message I am presenting, my "bad tone" becomes her open door for my rebuke. I'm sure I'm not the only guy who has been in the "dog house" or spent the night on the couch for popping off.

We have had whole nuclear meltdowns because of *how* I said something! It wasn't her problem; it was my problem!

We all need help in disarming the ticking bombs in our basement. Gentle words, a calm spirit, and a measured response are often the remedy for a peaceful resolution through difficult times.

One of the best stories in scripture, which validates this truth, is played out in 1 Samuel 25 (it would be helpful for you to read the whole chapter right now).

You just know this chick got the short end of the stick when she settled for this guy.

Nabal, while a successful businessman, does not necessarily exude overflowing social graces or intelligence. When David's men come calling, Nabal is rude and lacking proper respect. Now he has pissed off the (already anointed) next King of Israel for Heaven's sake! Not good! So David grabs his sword, commissions 400 commandos, and rides off to have a little "meet your Maker" meeting with the very stupid and idiotic Nabal.

Ever seen a couple together and wonder, "How the frik did *he* get *her*?" I see it all the time! Hell, you may be saying that about me!

Elegant, serious, classy women who have attached themselves to little boys who refuse to be men and will not put away their toys or grow the heck up! It is a stinking ridiculous epidemic inside our self-centered culture of entitlement!

This "boy" Nabal is dumber than a bag of hammers!

I literally weep under the emotion around verses 23-31. The breath of God flows through Abigail.

She acts, she repents, she owns—she falls at David's feet and her *"gentle answers"* diffuse his wrath. It is a stellar display of divine wisdom.

This stud chick shows us the value of real humility in speech. Some people have this amazing elastic heart that is able to stretch around those who do not deserve it. Her husband is spared (even though it is short lived) and the King elects to abstain from immediate bloodshed.

Abigail's actions and soft words accomplish a variety of blessings for everyone involved!

Of course, it did not end well for Abigail's husband. Nabal's story is a pathetic tale and he only had himself to blame. But Abigail is lifted up and promoted throughout the whole affair. She has astutely shown us the way to the riches of wisdom. He who has ears to hear, let him hear.

In The Pages

What other lessons have you learned by using gentle answers and soft responses? Review James 3:1-12. Does anything in there validate today's lesson? Explain.

Easy Button

January 16
Proverbs 16

"Mortals make elaborate plans, but God has the last word." Proverbs 16:1, MSG

"The mind of man plans his way, but the Lord directs his steps." Proverbs 16:9, NASB

"The steps of a man are established by the Lord, and He delights in his way. When he falls, he will not be hurled headlong, because the Lord is the One who holds his hand." Psalms 37:23-24, NASB

There is nothing in this that is a rebuke from Wisdom. It is just the way it is.

We get pretty wound up and lost in our plans and visions for what we want. Getting a plan is a good thing, but sometimes our plans and His plans are not dialed into the same wavelength. It could be that, from His perspective, there is a better way with a much more desired result, and it requires some tweaking by the Lord.

We get stressed out when our plans do not manifest the way we envisioned them playing out. We have strong ideas and passions around our plans. The problem is that we are limited in our vision.

But HE has unlimited vision. And if we have more confidence in our plans than simple trust in Him, His course corrections have the potential to derail our hopes.

God isn't required to stick with our business models for ministry. The immature are often bewildered and demand answers from God to the questions, *"Where is this going and why?"*

Be honest. Is it not our tendency to think that because a circumstance is hard that we must have missed God, or that we are headed in the wrong direction? Of course, there are always those who will automatically blame the devil. But most of us tend to blame ourselves:

"What did I do to deserve this?"

But beloved, have you considered the fact that because you ARE THE WILL OF GOD and because you ARE headed in the right direction, those things which are difficult and hard may just be the natural result of trying to do something good for God?

You are not being punished!

The verses in Psalms 37 indicate that there are days when we fall. We do not always get it right. We trip, we fail, we get confused, we feel lost, we cannot find God, we stress… we fall. But that does not mean we have missed God, does it?

On the contrary! The Lord has promised that He has our hand and He is committed to our finishing well and strong!

Disappointment is a great teacher, maybe the best. My own testimony is that failure has taught me more about life and ministry than success. I have worn a lot of smoke over the years, but none of those hardships disqualified me from ministry.

I know that God has been in most of those fires. We need to hold on to our plans and dreams, but understand that they **RARELY** happen exactly as we imagine.

We need to remember that God is refining our character through both victories

AND disappointments. He cares much more about that than any of our plans.

For Him to give us more authority or responsibility, without proper character, is recipe for disaster.

God knows what we need for our development. Stop assuming that hardship is a bad thing.

As my friend yells, "*Of course it's hard! That is what makes it great!*"[2]

Amen!

In The Pages

Are you under the impression that Christianity has an "easy button?" Why? Have you ever thought and hoped to be raptured out of hard? What was ever easy in Jesus' and the apostles' lives? How do you know if you are doing God's will? What has been the value of some hard things in your life?

Inside Job

January 17
Proverbs 17

"Better is a dry morsel with quietness, than a house full of feasting with strife." Proverbs 17:1, NKJV

Obviously the point is not about food. Wisdom is reminding us that the stress and agitation around strife, contention, disputes, lawsuits, adversarial relationships, controversies, and quarrels take their toll on us.

We do not wear our stress very well. We are probably the most self-medicated generation ever! Most of it is to help us deal with the effects of our stress.

Professional counselors and authors of self-help offerings have more than enough business. Their offices are packed with people. We do not rest well.

But how could we... rest... well?

Between Dr. Phil, Dr. Oz and Oprah, there is always another suggestion on how to do whatever we are doing better. We measure our looks by the magazines on the racks at the grocery store. We are constantly reminded our "stuff" needs to be replaced every time we turn on our television.

The divorce rates are climbing, suicide still happens, racism is still alive, catastrophes are happening left and right, sickos with guns still aim and shoot at the innocent, terrorism is real, the economy always sucks, chemicals in our food are killing us and supposedly, we are running out of water.

Damn. It's rough out there!

Most of our spiritual leaders are sincere, but they like the sound of their own voice way too much. And the prophets are constantly screaming at us that the "sky is falling" because of some governmental reform they do not agree with. Geez!

We have a desperate need for some peace in our lives! We are living on the edge and it doesn't appear that we are coping very well. Seriously, we need a little peace!

What are we to do?

We cannot fix it all. Sure, we can and should pray, but somewhere along the line we have to pull it together, gather the family, create some opportunity for rest and embrace those around us with some simple kindness and love.

A head-in-the-sand approach is not the suggestion here, but we can assess and monitor the amount of agitation we allow into our homes. This stuff affects us! And what affects us adults definitely touches our children.

If dad and mom fuss and fight about money, or whatever other nonsense we fight about, you can be assured it is messing with the kids.

Although we have limited power to change stuff "out there", we can make positive decisions about creating a peaceful and restful atmosphere at home. We can fill our abodes with music and messages of praise and worship.

Children can watch their parents love each other, speak respectfully and serve one another. We can leave our work at work and enter our homes and be family.

I seriously think that if we periodically fasted prime time television, talk radio, soap operas (that is the right description for them) and political talking heads for about 30 days, we would notice quite a bit of tension dissipate from our homes. Just saying.

It is all like electronic adrenalin on steroids! Some of that stuff only stirs stress.

Laugh if you want, label me if you must, but a little reflection here might lead you to some of the same conclusions.

Try a little quiet. See if the Peace doesn't come.

In The Pages

Read Philippians 4:1-9. Write down some of your thoughts concerning the Apostle's instructions. What can be applied in your own life, home, or church? Are you at odds with your mate right now? Is what you're contending over really worth the agitation in and around your home?

Accountability

January 18
Proverbs 18

"He who separates himself seeks his own desire, he quarrels against all sound wisdom." Proverbs 18:1, NASB

"In the spring, at the time when kings go off to war, David sent Joab out with the king's men and the whole Israelite army. They destroyed the Ammonites and besieged Rabbah. But David remained in Jerusalem. One evening David got up from his bed and walked around on the roof of the palace. From the roof he saw a woman bathing. The woman was very beautiful, and David sent someone to find out about her. The man said, "She is Bathsheba, the daughter of Eliam and the wife of Uriah the Hittite." 2 Samuel 11:1-3, NIV

I have often wondered just how much of his life story David shared with his son Solomon? How many of the details of his own mistakes did he use as a platform to teach the sound and deep truths of wisdom to his heir apparent? You just know that those fourteen words found in today's focus verse drips and oozes warnings for the young student.

I have these video images running through my mind of how lions hunt. Usually an entire pride hunts together and the goal is to separate out of a herd the desired target or victim. It isn't always the weakest or smallest member.

These predators are very clever, using every advantage they have to bring down animals that are bigger and extremely strong. They set traps, they'll drive the singled-out target into a desired area where they can gang up, dog-pile, go for the neck and kill their prey.

I can hear Peter's warning, *"Be sober, be vigilant; because your adversary the devil walks about like a roaring lion, seeking whom he may devour"* (1 Peter 5:8, NKJV).

When you explore this entire scenario concerning David and Bathsheba, the adultery, the murder of Uriah and the loss of a child, this whole sad saga begins with a serious problem at the onset of the story. To the point, David got himself isolated. He was not where he was supposed to be.

Temptations are everywhere. That is why we need accountability and purpose. For whatever reason, David elected to shun the duties that tracked with his authority.

"But David remained in Jerusalem." -Sigh-

So, there it is! The man is in the wrong place, at the wrong time, possibly bored and probably a little restless. Like a midnight stroll into the kitchen, hungry for a snack but not wanting a full meal, he examines and desires an exquisite yet forbidden morsel and unleashes the hounds of hell.

Nothing gets demonized in our lives quicker than a deeply hidden secret.

Of course, freedom and forgiveness for our sins is readily available, but the pain, the guilt and the shame we release upon our own heads, and the disappointment in the eyes of others, is absolutely devastating.

We need each other to help hold our feet to the fire. Accountability is a blessing, not a curse! This is why we need real, honest, bold community.

In The Pages

Please review Hebrews 10:23-25. Do you have a covenant friend who will risk offending you in order to remind you of a serious truth you need to hear? Do you have a secret that needs the light? Do you feel good about your levels of accountability? Why or why not?

Spoiled Trust

January 19
Proverbs 19

"Better to be poor and honest than a rich person no one can trust." Proverbs 19:1, MSG

"O Lord, I love the habitation of Your house and the place where Your glory dwells. Do not take my soul away along with sinners, nor my life with men of bloodshed, in whose hands is a wicked scheme, and whose right hand is full of bribes. But as for me, I shall walk in my integrity; redeem me, and be gracious to me." Psalms 26:8-11, NASB

When you heard the banging of those tiny timbrels and saw that the procession approaching from a distance included the nation's prophet, there had to be some anxiety. Was this going to be a good visit or a long afternoon?

Prophets did not make casual visits. These boys lived in remote obscurity until it was time to reveal some message from the heart of God. Unlike the former King, David welcomed such interruptions.

He too had a heart that longed to give expression to God's desires for himself and for Israel. Now sober and alert, David received his guest and settled in to do the ancient business of the prophets.

"Nathan then said to David, 'You are the man!'" (2 Samuel 12:7, NASB).

Black spots had to appear before his eyes. The room must have been spinning and surely sweat was beginning to seep through the royal robes. You know David did not take this lightly. The nausea, the guilt, the shame; it all came crashing around his sensitive spirit.

Everything that went down with Bathsheba had now come to light. The worst of it was, he knew again that God had seen it all... every naked bit of it.

This King, who had a passionate heart for the Lord, was now faced with coming to grips with the reality that he had sabotaged his own integrity and violated the trust of the nation.

All of his influence, and all the amassed power and wealth of the kingdom, could not fix this. Those things were useless to him now.

David had given permission to his enemies to taunt him, ridicule his administration, sneer at the kingdom and blaspheme his God. There was nothing left to do but admit his sin.

So he did—very quickly!

And his forgiveness was immediate. But the ultrasound of natural consequence continued to have its merciless way. The carnage was distinct and much too bloody, even for Israel's warrior King.

Solomon knew the truth. When you take a closer look, hindsight really is golden.

What good is it to have wealth and power if no one trusts you because of how you run the affairs of your own life?

Wealth does not provide immunity from such things. In fact, because you are royalty, it is mandated that integrity be one of your preeminent callings. Mulligans are just too expensive!

The entire theme of Psalm 26 is David's cry for vindication from his accusers. Bold statements revolve around the lessons David learned about deceit as well as the mistakes he made in assuming that wealth and power were automatically equated to righteousness.

Some things are much more valuable to us than financial gain. Honesty. Integrity. Having an upright heart that people can easily access and validate.

Those are the real things that determine the value of our lives.

In The Pages

See Psalm 26:2. What do you think David is asking? Have you ever asked God the same? How did that work out for you?

Self-Govern

January 20
Proverbs 20

"Wine is a mocker, strong drink a brawler, and whoever is intoxicated by it is not wise." Proverbs 20:1, NASB

"All things are lawful for me, but not all things are profitable. All things are lawful for me, but I will not be mastered by anything." I Corinthians 6:12, NASB

Almost everything that is good in our lives has the potential to become a bad thing if we are not able to manage a little bit of self-governance.

Wisdom is reminding us of a simple fact: if you drink too much wine, guzzle your beer, gulp your champagne, or ingest large quantities of liquor, it will jeopardize your ability to monitor your words and actions. You do that long enough and on a regular basis; you may find that you cannot stop. Soon, you could find yourself stuck in destructive patterns that make your life miserable and odious to others.

Alcohol is the example here, but the list of things that can do this to us is very long! Wisdom says intoxication is not a good thing. Paul boasts that he doesn't allow anything in his life to "manage" him except for Christ.

Yes, too much booze does elevate the risk of losing our faculties and our witnesses. But is the real problem the wine, *or* the lack of responsible stewardship?

Depending on what system you find yourself in, there is always a short list of what defiles you. Many Christians around the world chuckle at American evangelicals who rant about the evils of alcohol.

For most Catholics, the notion is inconceivable! The Benedictines have long brewed the best ales and liqueurs in the world! Jesus said, *"It is not what enters into the mouth that defiles the man, but what proceeds out of the mouth, this defiles the man"* (Matthew 15:11, NASB).

Naturally, religious folks in certain camps are going to be offended by this, just like the Pharisees were in Matthew 15:12. But we need to really "hear" Him here.

Our tendency is to observe the externals, and then make judgments about the internals. Jesus was rarely "put-off" by the outside stuff. He always moved straight to the heart of the matter.

IF you cannot handle drinking, then DO NOT drink!

If your addictive-compulsive behavior is best served by not drinking, or if you have a family history littered with alcoholics, then do yourself and everyone else a favor, and **DO NOT DRINK!**

Make good choices about that kind of stuff! But stay open-minded to the possibility that not all drinking leads to intoxication for everyone! Because you saw your daddy get drunk and beat the hell out of your momma, doesn't mean that is the standard out there.

Not all love is lustful, not all sex is porn, using drugs does not always trigger addiction (I'm pretty thankful for Novocain while the dentist is grinding on my molars!), and a good meal with a rich dessert does not necessarily make you a viable candidate for "The Biggest Loser."

Just because something is a devil to me, does not mean that it is automatically a devil to you.

If it is not profitable to you, then just say "no thank you." Real freedom is always about what you "ought" to do.

Irresponsibility is not the kind of freedom we seek!

In The Pages

Unhealed wounds of rejection can provide the platforms of bondages that entrap our lives. What are you doing to get healed? Is it working? Are you living free or are you medicating pain? What has you?

I certainly realize that addiction can be a serious problem. I also understand that it's quite often much more complicated than just deciding not to drink, smoke, shoot up, or snort what narcotizes our pain, wounds, or needs. The point here is not to condemn. Please know that! The hope here is that we'd all honestly assess our situation and proactively move towards our freedom and ultimate health. Professional and spiritual help is out there if we're hung and need real help. It requires incredible courage to own the truth of our situation. May the Lord grant us the grace to walk in total freedom and His loving peace.
—MDP 2018

Bad Grits

January 21
Proverbs 21

"The king's heart is in the hand of the LORD, like the rivers of water; He turns it wherever He wishes." Proverbs 21:1, NKJV

Yes, someone has to do it. But why would anyone actually *want* to be the president of the United States of America?

Whoever wins the election has already made enemies of nearly half the population. It is the ultimate no-win position.

Sure, a tragedy or national disaster releases the unspoken gravitational pull towards temporary unity and bipartisanship, but, when it is back to "business as usual", the political pressure of public opinion and the ever-present weight of responsibility must be crushing!

"Party-line people" are hired to either spin and polish every idea, or seek and destroy, with dissecting precision, each word the man speaks. Everyone weighs in. Turn on the television, grab a paper or tune in to the radio. It's a free-for-all out there!

And it's not real clear that anyone is even winning. Hindsight, maybe 20 to 50 years later, is the only thing that can really be trusted to determine with any real accuracy the historical legacy and value of the President.

We really do need to do a better job of praying for the men and women who hold office in our governmental affairs. It is a terribly awesome responsibility.

Chicken Little has nothing on most Christians' fears about the demise of our nation. If *our* guy was not elected or *our* cause is not being met with the attention we think it deserves, we react in a way which embarrassingly shows how riddled with fear we really are.

The Apostle Paul reminded the men and women in the church at Rome,

"Every person is to be in subjection to the governing authorities. For there is no authority except from God, and those which exist are established by God" (Romans 13:1, NASB).

It is a simple reminder from the apostle that God has not abandoned us because of Health Care Legislation, or any other kind of legislation for that matter.

I once heard Pastor Peter Lord say in a sermon in my church, *"We think God likes grits because we like grits."*[3] Just because the President leads in a way that is contrary to our opinions doesn't make him the anti-Christ does it?

No doubt, there is corruption in our government. But it is not all bad. We need to push past this fear-plagued panic over our President and nation.

Pray for that man. Pray for his wife and his children. Bless them with your words. Vote for your candidate, plead for your causes, and take action on the things that matter to you. Be proactive. But tearing down the man with your words does not change a thing, except the condition inside of your own heart.

One last thought: even if all the decisions that our president influences are bad for America, it still does not change the fact that God sits on His throne. We should be wary of "doom and gloom prophecy" spoken over our country in fear.

Our God is a good God.
(Come on... say Amen! You know you want to!)

We may go through some fires in our future, but He will purify us and refine a people that will do His will no matter what.

President Roosevelt said, *"We have nothing to fear, but fear itself."*[4] Jesus promised to never leave us or forsake us. That is good news, my friend. Good news.

In The Pages

How do you respond when you hear ugly remarks about our nation's leaders? Read 1 Peter 2:11-17. What are some key thoughts for us to consider in this passage?

Names

January 22
Proverbs 22

"A good name is to be more desired than great wealth, favor is better than silver and gold." Proverbs 22:1, NASB

God lets life touch us. Things happen. We make mistakes. We get caught up in secrets and silence, and things that are not good for us suddenly show up in our lives like dandelions sprinkled throughout a thick bed of manicured Bermuda grass.

And we think, *how did this happen? How did this spin out of control so quickly?*

Why does bad news travel so fast? Are some things just too rich and too juicy not to talk about? I've heard it said more than once that the Church is the only army that shoots its own wounded.

Fallen preachers, deacons and leaders will never escape their soiled names and reputations. Lady Wisdom knows her history all too well. There is always some chilling experience "back there" that needs to warn us today. So it moved Wisdom's pen long ago.

I picture her shaking violently. Uncontrollably shaking. Hair a mottled mess, smeared lipstick, ultra thick eye paint, barely clothed, scared, exposed, standing on a dusty road that is now slightly darkened near her feet by her own urine mingled with the body fluids of her secret lover.

Angry men scream at her, threaten her; they spit at her tear-soaked face. She is dragged from the shadows into the light to stand trial in front of Galilee's new wonder boy. Of course, she stands alone. She is (*whisper*) *"the adulterer."*

Now how does that work again? Were there not two people involved here? Wonder where he slithered off to?

Of course, they all know *her* name. Everyone knows *her* name. She wears shame like a neon tramp stamp. That was no secret. It was never really a secret.

They all knew where she lived, how she operated and what was "offered" over at that house. It would have been a good day not to have a name.

But she did have a name.

It wasn't worth a damn, but everyone knew her name.

Once Jesus stood and looked at her accusers, it was over. Like a skilled surgeon, He peeled back their flesh to reveal a sad rottenness lying deep within their own dead religious bones.

No one got to throw their rock that day. Such a pity. According to their Law, they were right and He was... was... confusing as hell.

Few heard His words to this bedraggled soul. *"Woman,"* he begins (John 8:10). It was the same word he used to address his own mother from the cross (John 19:26). One look from Him was enough to split you wide open.

That one word packed a million messages. With that little loving salutation, He changed her name. He changed her life.

She was no longer "_____, the adulterer"; "_____, the slut"; or "_____, the cheating whore." Nothing of the sorts. She was forgiven, absolved, and given a fresh start.

That is what He does and that is what He will do. There is much to celebrate in this truth.

We are not what we *do right* or what we have *done wrong*.

You are not Bill the addict; Sally the drunk; Paul the racist; Tommy the pervert; James the liar; Mike the coward; June the anorexic; Donna the control freak; Stan the porno king; or Pam the divorcee.

NONE of those things are on His lips! These are not the names HE calls you and me!

We ARE who and what He calls us:
BELOVED
ACCEPTED
BLESSED
CHOSEN
FRIEND
HEIR
SON
DAUGHTER
ROYALTY
CHILD

He does want to touch all of those other things that rape and hide our true self, and He will if you allow Him to do so, but first find His loving heart. He can and will change your name.

In The Pages

Has He changed your name? How so? Write out your praise and thanks for His confronting your accusers. What does He call you?

Chew

January 23
Proverbs 23

"When you go out to dinner with an influential person, mind your manners:

don't gobble your food, don't talk with your mouth full. And don't stuff yourself; bridle your appetite." Proverbs 23:1-3, MSG

I love Eugene Peterson's version of this text. It makes me laugh.

The reason is that I grew up just a couple blocks from where I went to Jr. High and High School. We had about 30 minutes for lunch and, with about 15 minutes travel time by foot, that gave you about 10 minutes to eat if you were planning on brushing your teeth after the meal.

There was no time for conversation or any real enjoyment of the intake process. It was "shovel and swallow."

With eyes watering and ears ringing, the whole process was a blur until you hit the street back to school. My wife says I am still hung in that loop.

I can eat a whole double cheeseburger before she even gets her Jr. burger unwrapped. And, IF I am really hungry, it is just downright ugly.

"Where is the fire? Breathe! What's the rush?" If she does not remind me often, the race is on without my even realizing what I'm doing.

This is another one of those "self-awareness" talks the people who care for us sometimes need to risk in the name of love. People who are properly trained in manners and have been exposed to cultured protocol notice these things.

If a guy is being a pig at the table and *I* notice, it must be *really* bad.

Wisdom is pointing out that little things like manners at the table make an impression. Wisdom wants our voice and influence welcomed everywhere.

Wisdom says it is better to make sure that everyone is served before you. (Please read that last sentence one more time).

It is better to leave the table a little hungry rather than have people talk behind your back about what and how much you ate for supper.

My wife is my toughest critic about this kind of stuff. It's not because she is trying to shame me or embarrass me, but she honestly desires for people to want to be around me. I want that also, and I need to be reminded that bad first impressions are hard to erase.

Food is such a social affair, and we need to use some caution as to how we handle ourselves around the table. It is a great place to connect and establish deep rapport with new friends and associates. Wisdom suggests that we be extremely aware and intentional in all of our affairs.

The table is no exception.

In The Pages

As I child, do you remember ever getting into trouble at the table? What was the cause? Do you know what to do at the most elegant of settings in a classy restaurant? If asked, do you know how to open a bottle of wine or champagne for a celebration? Would it hurt to read up and refresh a bit on those details?

Real Help

January 24
Proverbs 24

"Do not be envious of evil men, nor desire to be with them; for their minds devise violence, and their lips talk of trouble." Proverbs 24:1-2, NASB

"For their heart studieth destruction, and their lips talk of mischief." Proverbs 24:2, KJV

I can still hear my mom's voice echoing in the back of my head as she tells my 11-year-old self, *"We do not associate with those kind of people!"* I just thought the kid was cool because he smoked cigarettes, had some dirty magazines and an older girlfriend that he smooched a lot at the skating rink.

I mean, of course those things are appealing to an innocent pubescent. Growing up, I was given more than enough fishing line to swim within certain protected boundaries. But whenever I started giving off the stench of arrogance or pride, mom would set the hook like fisherman Bill Dance when the camera is rolling.

Kids need a good reeling in every now and then. Thanks mom!

The King's language version of this verse messes with me. *"Their heart studieth destruction."* It was a concentrated, calculated observation and examination of how to destroy themselves and others; motivated intention to bring negative influence and harm.

The world can be such an ugly place sometimes. Some people have so much destruction going on in their lives that they are just not reachable by our talking or intervention. Our presence does not sway them. Sometimes the only thing we can do is pray and stay out of the process.

God is capable of breaking them and bringing about productive life-altering change. We are eager to step in because we know of a healthier way to live, but prayer may actually be the only thing that we can insert into their environment. This is really tough when it is a son or a daughter, a close friend or a parent.

Maybe you have talked until you are blue in the face and it is just not registering. They are flat out stiff-arming you. It is brutally painful to be drafted into this kind of mischief, loved one or not.

One of the couples most responsible for teaching Patti and I how to really pray for people in bondage taught us that sometimes, you flat-out have to let people go. That means loving them enough to actually let them lick some of the world's dirt and eat the garbage off the streets, in hopes that one day they will have had enough of that slop and ask for real help.

Until people cross that threshold and really see the destruction in their way, there really isn't any strategy you can use. They have to hit that wall.

Once they hit that wall, then we can all kick in and do what we can to help. But until then, it might be better to keep your distance, all the while loving, praying and believing for something better.

In The Pages

Who is breaking your heart? Can you imagine their hell and understand their pain? It has been said that God's judgment *is* actually His mercy. What are your thoughts about that?

Influence

January 25
Proverbs 25

"These also are proverbs of Solomon which the men of Hezekiah, king of Judah, transcribed." Proverbs 25:1, NASB

If my math serves me correctly, there are 137 verses that follow today's text in

Proverbs, all compiled by Hezekiah's influence, yet all are attributed to Solomon. The reason I point that out is because Hezekiah didn't come into power for another 215 years after Solomon's death.

Conventional Bible chronology has Solomon's death around 931 B.C., and Hezekiah's sole reign as king of Judah beginning in 716 B.C. Considering the fact that Hezekiah didn't have a Bible in his possession, and quite a bit of time had elapsed since Solomon's reign, it's amazing that Hezekiah orchestrated such diligence for this work.

Granted, the oral traditions of Israel were tediously thorough, yet the tireless work of subservient scribes recorded every word, thought and movement of the ruling class. That wasn't really anything new.

What I do want to point out is the influence Solomon's life had on those around him and that his life still influences us, even all these years after his death.

Business and life coaches regularly point out that influence and leadership are so deeply intermingled that you can't really separate them. If you can influence people, you can lead.

If you're a leader, you already have at least some influence; otherwise no one would be following you. Yes, a world leader such as Solomon is definitely going to influence people, but *how* he influenced and the legacy of equity and wisdom he left behind is what separates him from his contemporaries.

Unlike Saul and David, who were "anointed" into their offices and both endowed with charismatic favor, Solomon inherited his reign. He was the first of Israel's dynasty kings. And his love affair with wisdom left a significant mark on the world.

He acquired wisdom, but he also operated in wisdom. That is what made him legendary. Heck, he administrated the transition of Israel from a tribal confederacy to a strong, centralized government. He ruled without ever having to wage any major military campaign. That alone is astonishing!

Of course, his building the Temple in Jerusalem was the jewel in his crown of acclaim. He wasn't perfect, but overall, the guy was a stud!

So, what was it about Solomon that gave him so much influence over everyone and everything?

Short answer: WISDOM

No one had ever done things the way Solomon did them. Sure, his pops had influence with him, but Solomon had a way of taking the good things and making them great!

Wisdom was a significant player in all of that. From his toes he oozed the stuff, and that greatness is still rocking the globe today.

So what about you? The take-away for today is that legacy is all about our influence. What legacy do you want to leave behind?

What values do you want to instill in the people around you now? Which of your characteristics will continue to influence your family after you are gone? Will you be known to following generations as a person who lived honorably, full of the Holy Spirit, committed to Kingdom, a respecter of wisdom and a lover of all?

Wisdom will help with the strategy, but you have to have the courage to live it from the heart.

In The Pages

What do you admire most about Solomon? List the top five attributes of influence that you want written about your life in the next 100 years. Ask the Lord to help make it so!

Who Ya Fooling?

January 26
Proverbs 26

"We no more give honors to fools than pray for snow in summer or rain during harvest." Proverbs 26:1, MSG

I do not know the first thing about farming, other than what I picked up from the local hayseeds around my hometown. But I suspect that snow in the summer is really bad during growing season, and rain during harvest makes farmers say bad words. In other words, no farmer is hoping for such a thing.

Farming has gotten to be such an exact science with all its complicated strategies. Don't let the slow talking and overalls fool you. Farmers are some of the brightest and most unshakable people among us.

There is all this due diligence that farmers are constantly attending to with their crops and fields. But Mother Nature is not something they have very much control over. They can hedge their bets a bit, with irrigation and pesticides—but a tall midsummer hailstorm, nasty tornado; flood or drought can wipe out a healthy crop very easily.

So I reckon that the boys who have been in this business a long time know how to hope and pray for needed rain, warm nights and a good, dry window to get the fruit of their labors into the market.

I cannot see a farmer doing what he does without some interaction with the Creator of all nature's processes and growing things. It would be foolish not to. The word *"fool"* in Proverbs refers to a person who is a doofus: *"someone who is stupid or a dullard."* Yeah, it's pretty brutal.

It's not just about ignorance, because ignorance may be due to a lack of proper education or even the inability to learn. A fool knows better, but for whatever reason refuses or ignores responsible attitudes and actions about life and others.

Ecclesiastes 4:5 says that the fool is more than capable of doing what is right, but makes the choice to consume or eat their own flesh, rather than exercise prudence with their gifts and abilities. It's a picture of a person who has become completely absorbed with his or her "self," but at the same time, has lost all self-awareness (how people really see us).

They have lost touch with the "reality" around them. Sometimes we can't see our own crap without the help of another voice. Like David, we need a Nathan to point it out to us.

Remember, we probably "know" better and have the understanding to make the necessary adjustments. But do we still ask for respect and honor when we are not living up to all of our responsibilities?

In The Pages

Sir, are you recognized in your home for your spirituality? Have you earned that honor and is it lovingly given by all; or is it just something you demand and everyone else just tolerates your religious games?

Madame, are you stewarding all of your God-given charms, beauties and loving graces in conveying your love and trust to your husband? Can you answer without a long list of excuses?

As "children," do you still honor your parents? Would your parents agree? Why or why not?

Time

January 27
Proverbs 27

"Do not boast about tomorrow, for you do not know what a day may bring forth." Proverbs 27:1, NASB

"Don't brashly announce what you're going to do tomorrow; you don't know the first thing about tomorrow." Proverbs 27:1, MSG

Franciscan priest Richard Rohr often says, *"All great spirituality is about letting go."*[5] It is a direct challenge to the amount of control we "Christians" try to have over everything. But the control we think we have is all just a fancy illusion.

We make our plans, we manipulate people around us and we take charge in probably way too many things. I do not think that Wisdom is taking issue with our iCals or our Day-Timers. The problem is that we get so involved, so focused, so consumed with doing our "deals," that we forget we have a spiritual element to our lives.

God is not just some cosmic ideal that sets our standards of morality and exists only in theological theory and not our daily practicalities.

God is Spirit, but He's also personal and tangible.

We can have a *relationship* with Him. I mean, like a real relationship. And that relationship can be carried with us into every nook and cranny of our lives. He is so much more than having something to do on Sundays.

Take a close look at James 4:13-16:

Come now, you who say, "Today or tomorrow we will go to such and such a city, spend a year there, buy and sell, and make a profit"; whereas you do not know what will happen tomorrow. For what is your life? It is even a vapor that appears for a little time and then vanishes away. Instead you ought to say, "If the Lord wills, we shall live and do this or that." But now you boast in your arrogance. All such boasting is evil" (NIV).

Evil? Yes, evil as in diseased character evil. Frik!

Pastor James is passionately reminding his flock that they need to stop acting like they are in control of time and existence. People were going about their chores and running their errands like God had no say about anything in their lives.

James was making a bold attempt to get them to see that their faith in Christ needed to be integrated into every facet of their day. People were scurrying around, anxious, nervous and stressed, making plans for another day, all without even considering that tomorrow is not promised to anyone. Sound familiar?

There is nothing wrong with planning and casting vision, but if you can't be in "today" because of your worries about tomorrow, you need to back the trolley up a bit. Really, we need to chill the hell out and examine how much of today we are really living in.

In The Pages

Read Psalms 90:12. How does this passage correlate to what we talked about today? Read Matthew 6:25-34. Do you believe that you live in this kind of reality? What is pulling on you now that has you totally distracted today, about tomorrow?

If there is anything that writing **TIL DEATH DO US PART** *taught Patti and myself is that tomorrow is a mystery. Anything from this moment right now, moving forward, is not guaranteed. So, kiss again if you can, hug again if you can, love again if you can, and say "I'm sorry" if it needs to be said. Make right now important. —MDP 2018*

Run Forrest, Run!

January 28
Proverbs 28

"The wicked are edgy with guilt, ready to run off even when no one's after them; honest people are relaxed and confident, bold as lions." Proverbs 28:1, MSG

Take a big ole deep breath and read that passage one more time. Relaxed. Confident. Bold. Yes Lord!

After my three-year stint in coaching and public education, I moved back to the area where I had grown up and went to work for my father's insurance business. I struggled at first but eventually I got my license, began making local contacts, writing small policies and just generally pestered all my old friends for their business. As I grew in confidence and experience, I started setting up appointments with potentially larger clients.

Near my hometown, there was a large company that manufactured road construction products. They had a sizable number of employees and the potential for a sale was promising.

I had made an appointment with the representative of the business, showed up on time, made all the proper introductions and was about to enter into my contact's office when suddenly, two large pastel-green buses pulled into the yard to block the front gate. At the same time, a helicopter appeared out of nowhere and was circling the facility. It was the border patrol making a surprise visit to the plant.

Evidently, the bulk of the employees were illegal immigrants. The place went into frenzied panic! I stared at the scene like it was some kind of old Godzilla film. Men were running everywhere! I mean, full on sprinting! Running for their lives!

People were falling down, climbing fences, and trying to get away as fast as they could. An unmanned and moving forklift is a crazy thing to watch plow into stacks of new product. It felt like slow-motion chaos!

The office staff was horrified. I had to inquire because I was still in shock. It seems when the illegals started running, everyone in the yard started running as well. Yeah, everyone!

My contact explained, *"Not everyone is a model citizen out there. Guess their first impression is that someone or some 'thing' is always after them."*

It was funny at the time and we all shared a reluctant giggle, but that comment is certainly relevant to today's text.

In all sincerity, I don't think it's always the "big things" that unsettle our heart. Most of us know enough truth to realize that if we commit big crimes, we pay big consequences.

I get why the illegal immigrant workers ran. We usually always run and cover up when we are doing things we are not supposed to be doing. Even the small things can make us coy as well.

We have to remember that the voice that talked us into our error is the exact same voice that will turn and condemn us with shame and overall rotten feelings when it is all said and done.

That's how darkness rolls.

In The Pages

Read Colossians 3:12-17. Record the thoughts in your mind that speak to sensible and peaceful living.

Stubborn

January 29
Proverbs 29

"He who is often rebuked, and hardens his neck, will suddenly be destroyed, and that without remedy." Proverbs 29:1, NKJV

I do not know why, but this verse is gut wrenching to me. Something that has the potential to help, steer or disciple another person through possible treacherous waters ends up being the source of a wound or an offense. It is essential to remember that how we rebuke is important. There is more going on than just the message.

How another person receives a rebuke has plenty to do with the spirit in which we deliver our packages of truth or correction. I guess this is the pastor in me burping forth, but men and women who have pastoral duties, have a responsibility to rebuke in a spirit of redemptive quality.

"I solemnly charge you in the presence of God and of Christ Jesus, who is to judge the living and the dead, and by His appearing and His kingdom: preach the word; be ready in season and out of season; reprove, rebuke, exhort, **with great patience and instruction***. For the time will come when they will not endure sound doctrine; but wanting to have their ears tickled, they will accumulate for themselves teachers in accordance to their own desires, and will turn away their ears from the truth and will turn aside to myths"* (2 Timothy 4:1-4, NASB).

The purpose is not to wound, but to give correction and instruction. Keep in mind, however, that sometimes, no matter how you deliver the message, the hearer is bound to be offended. That person is in jeopardy of getting themself in trouble with the Lord, as our focus verse today points out.

There is always an opportunity for repentance, forgiveness and reconciliation. But the warning here is about plain ole stiff-necked stubbornness.

Either pride has kicked in, or self-pity has had its way. There is a horrible seriousness in this. Having been in many "church" type environments, I am convinced that no matter what system or denomination a person is in, most have made a sincere choice to really belong.

Most are trying to find God and follow the teachings of the faith. We get zealous and set in our patterns and may even have a specific passion about something that is really close to our heart.

It is easy to get possessive and protective about our beliefs and to what we actively give our money and ourselves. But what happens when we are approached, challenged and corrected by our spiritual leaders?

What occurs when we flat-out don't get our way on something at our church?

There is a wilderness out there, full of people who no longer choose to participate in church because of past strained relationships at church. There is no hurt like church hurt!

And people are not perfect, including pastors. But once an offense becomes a wound, it can release bitterness, judgment and stubbornness towards God and His people. It benefits no one, especially the person who was originally wounded.

How many marriages end because of stubbornness? How many children left home too young and never went back because of their wounding and stubbornness?

How many neighbors actually dislike each other because of some stupid thing that happened 20 or 30 years ago? We need help in this area. Someone has to be the first to repent and ask for forgiveness.

Yeah, someone.

In The Pages

Read Matthew 5:23-24. Why do you think Jesus nailed us with this teaching? Imagine the finger of God poking into your chest cavity. If He is going to touch your stubbornness button, what will He find out (yeah, He already knows all about it)?

Power Demon

January 30
Proverbs 30

"If you're dumb enough to call attention to yourself by offending people and making rude gestures, don't be surprised if someone bloodies your nose. Churned milk turns into butter; riled emotions turn into fist fights." Proverbs 30:32-33, MSG

"But now you also, put them all aside: anger, wrath, malice, slander, and abusive speech from your mouth." Colossians 3:8, NASB

I have never been a person who enjoys confrontation. Some people seem to thrive on the agitation, but not me.

As a child, because of the amount of fear I had in my life, I would do just about anything to avoid a conflict or a fight. Just the thought of a possible "show down" with another person was enough to make me nauseous.

Now, my position as a leader in the Body of Christ requires me to handle people and their problems in delicate fashion. It requires firmness, strong words and muscled ideas. But allowing anger into that process is unacceptable.

There have been times when I have been angry and developed preconceived notions about how to handle certain situations. But when I took the issue to the Lord, any desire for an ugly outburst was quickly diffused and replaced with something much more graceful.

It happens that way almost every time!

Too often, anger is used as a "power" to push or manipulate a situation. At the core, we are afraid of not getting our way.

Fear creeps in when we realize something feels like it's spinning out of our control. So we use anger to force someone else into doing what we want.

An angry person is a wounded and fearful person. We've all had things happen in our lives that give opportunity to vent anger. But we need to consider all the facets of what is really happening, or what is about to happen.

If we allow anger to have its way with us, Wisdom tells us what we can expect. Does anger really give us the result we want? There is another way.

Paul tells us in Colossians to *"put away"* angry speech along with other destructive attitudes. That is part of the solution, but we also need to deal with the anger in our hearts towards that person or problem. It usually requires our getting a different perspective.

How does God see the issue? Do I have ALL the facts? Have I taken offense and now stubbornly refuse to forgive and release?

It is so easy to blow our witness when we allow anger to have its way. We need help from the Lord to offer a proper response from our heart and mouth.

In The Pages

When was the last time you really lost your temper? Was it justifiable? What happened in your spirit after the fact? Read Proverbs 15:1. Paraphrase in your own words the truth of that passage.

Sobriety

January 31
Proverbs 31

"It is not for kings, O Lemuel, it is not for kings to drink wine, or for rulers to desire strong drink, for they will drink and forget what is decreed, and pervert the rights of all the afflicted." Proverbs 31:4-5, NASB

It feels like a bit of a contradiction. A little background might help a bit.

We think (scholars are not absolutely sure) that Lemuel was actually Solomon, and Bathsheba (Solomon's natural mother) is the voice of wisdom in this proverb. So we have a mother who is pouring her heart into a son with big-time social, political and religious responsibilities.

She hits two main topics: the importance of responsible sobriety while in leadership and the attentive realization that leaders make decisions that affect people.

The book of Proverbs is full of all kinds of warnings to consider our ways when we are responsible for others. The words of Wisdom here are truth.

Whatever might be the deterrent to sensible and heightened awareness when engaged in the affairs of headship, our stewardship of such duties has a direct effect on the lives of the people we serve. It demands that we be at our highest and best place of consciousness for the welfare of those we lead.

Mom's plea to her son is to remain sober while engaged in his duties, to not be careless or reckless while attending to state affairs. The public's trust is at stake, and if the people have reason to lose confidence in their leader, that trust is next to impossible to gain back.

I seriously doubt that Solomon abstained from using alcohol in every occasion, but I don't think that was the entire point of Wisdom's advice.

A part of the Law that we read in Exodus 23:1-9 gives us insight into what God thought about anyone who used personal and political power for individual gain via bribes and under-the-table dealings (*perverting the rights of all the afflicted*). A leader who relinquishes his duties by any kind of personal irresponsibility usurps his own authority.

Authority tracks with responsibility and responsibility tracks with authority.

We expect and trust our leaders to do their jobs to the best of their abilities. That is why Wisdom implores leaders to a sensibility that thinks beyond *me—here—right now*.

It is a great lesson we need on multiple levels.

In The Pages

What was the best practical advice given to you by your mom or mother figure? If applied, how has it benefited you? What is your general opinion of how leaders over you handle the levels of responsibility given to them? What kind of response pours from you in regards to those opinions?

Hear O, (fill in the blank)

February 1
Proverbs 1

"My son, hear the instruction of your father, and do not forsake the law of your mother; for they will be a graceful ornament on your head, and chains about your neck." Proverbs 1:8-9, NKJV

It was a big deal when you got the word *"hear"* in Wisdom literature. The Shema, *"Hear, O Israel: The Lord our God, the Lord is one"* (Deuteronomy 6:4, NKJV) was the basic confession of Judaism.

The name is derived from **shâma'** (pronounced *shaw-mah'*), meaning, *"to hear with your intellect and give attention to its truth with the intent to obey."* All kinds of bells went off to the severity and importance of what you were going to be told.

So Solomon's instruction focused on the one-two punch: dad's commandments and mother's enforcement of those commandments; also known as truth and law.

I don't want to distract from my path today, but a lot of people can relate to that notion of dad issuing the commands, and mom policing the action. That was kind of the way it was in the home where I grew up, so it was very important to *hear* on the front end, in order to avoid confrontation on the back end, if you get my drift.

Very little happens in the Body of Christ without our finding a way to attach a label to it and properly catalog the experience. For example, we can't just hang out in worship, waiting to hear what the Lord might have to say. We have to call it something, so we label it Harp and Bowl.

Then we develop a curriculum about how to orchestrate Harp and Bowl. Then, once we have a curriculum, we write books about Harp and Bowl.

If we have enough interest in that topic, then we put on a conference and bring in big-name speakers to talk about Harp and Bowl worship.

I often wonder if God ever looks down on all our activity and scratches His Holy head?

I doubt David ever called it anything. He just went into the Holy place to hang out and be near HIM. The hearing happened because of that.

I know there are all kinds of operations of intercession. The surfacing value and strategic roll of intercessors has drastically increased in the last 20 years. Even though prayer in itself is not a new concept, the *way* of intercessors and their role in the Body has taken on new forms and powerful strategies.

I have total appreciation for the relevance and importance of Spirit-led intercession! But, when you really get to the meat of prayer, you have to understand the importance of being able to *hear* the voice of the Holy Spirit.

In fact, the very core of prayer is being able to hear, not all the blabbing.

Have you ever tried to comfort or counsel someone who is wounded and won't shut up long enough for you to try to tell them something? Honestly, it is exhausting trying to respond in the midst of all that! We do that with our prayer sometimes.

There is no new information you can tell God. He already knows all about what you are burdened with. He knows your need before you ask. So, go ahead and ask. He'll be glad you asked. We are invited to ask! But we need to spend way more time listening rather than running our mouths.

Hearing or listening is not a style of prayer — ***IT IS PRAYER***! You may have a counter-argument... so... go ahead. I'm listening.

In The Pages

When you pray, are you a listener or a teller? Do you have an outlet for sharing what you believe you are hearing from God? How are you doing with your journal?

Lori Darling

February 2
Proverbs 2

"Who's faithless to the husband she married years ago, never gave a second thought to her promises before God. Her whole way of life is doomed; every step she takes brings her closer to hell. No one who joins her company ever comes back, ever sets foot on the path to real living." Proverbs 2:17-19, MSG

I guess the Lord wanted to give a jumpstart to my thinking this morning. Before I even crawled out of bed, I believe I heard the Lord say something to me about people whose lives just seem to miss the mark.

It could have been due to the fact that I finished watching Larry McMurtry's *Lonesome Dove* for the third time last night. It's an epic western about a couple of ex-Texas Rangers who move a large herd of cattle from the south Texas border to Montana.

The story is laced with sub-plots involving bad guys, soiled women, dangerous Indians and lots of cowboy philosophy. I'm pretty sure I wasn't tough enough to live back in those days!

It could be that Augustus McCrae's love of a prostitute named Lori Darling sparked my need to hear something righteously true from our Great Lover: *"I love the prostitute. I love the villain. I love the hardcore. I dislike their way which causes so much pain for themselves and for others, but I love them all."*

It is a major challenge for the Body of Christ to love like God loves.

I don't think we are too good at it. It's easier to front out the sin and condemn the person involved. We can do that without really even thinking about what we're doing.

The religion in us can manifest faster than we can say, "whore." Jesus' little talk on specks and logs really is a major challenge for us.

We should take the warning in today's text seriously. Whoever joins company with an adulterer is asking for lots of trouble. Whoever joins company with anyone or anything that isn't at least making an attempt at clean living is casting well-being to the wind. These warnings come from the very heart of wisdom, and we definitely need to pay attention.

I guess 30+ years of being a pastor has sobered me some about the ways of man. I don't think you could tell me a tale that would shock my understanding about human nature.

No matter what kind of cock-and-bull story I've heard, I don't believe that the Lord has ever permitted me to be a voice of condemnation to the person suffering with a problem. I'm not saying that I have never been condemning! I have been at times and my rotten judgment has always gotten in the way of me being able to really help another person.

What I'm saying is that, no matter what kind of situation I've had to stare down in another person's life, it was never okay for me to be condemning of their sin or error. Love doesn't just excuse another person's misdeeds, it actually makes an attempt to find the cause, hear the story, embrace that person and hold on until forgiveness comes.

Lori Darling is one of the most endearing characters in that whole movie. Sometimes I think Hollywood sees much more clearly than the church.

In The Pages

How are you doing in your relationships with people who don't value what you value? How did Jesus act around sinners? Cite some examples. Honestly, who did Jesus have the most problems with on this earth?

Heart Bottom

February 3
Proverbs 3

"Trust in the Lord with all your heart and lean not on your own understanding; in all your ways acknowledge him, and he will make your paths straight." Proverbs 3:5-6, NIV

"Trust God from the bottom of your heart; don't try to figure out everything on your own. Listen for God's voice in everything you do, everywhere you go; he's the one who will keep you on track." Proverbs 3:5-6, MSG

I hear these verses quoted quite a bit. At times, it sounds like we (people who love and serve God) are to check intellect and reason like you would check your overcoat at a fancy restaurant. People get paralyzed waiting on a word from God.

Hesitation in a busy intersection isn't a good thing. I can see how some religious folk, without really digging into the text, might assume that without a word from the Lord or a Bible verse in our pockets, it's best to stay in the parking lot. I don't think that's what Solomon is suggesting here.

The fact that God has given us a free will to make choices and decisions for our lives demands that we use our faculties. It is also the only way we can actually validate our love for God—the fact that we have *chosen* to love Him.

There are some bright people in this world who understand and apply great knowledge to benefit mankind. But I would assume that no matter what man achieves in his understanding, there is always a higher intellect—a master designer who is personal, aware and is willing to help us do our lives if we will just ask.

We are free to either involve God or not. Solomon suggests it would be wise to include Him.

I made a direct but casual inquiry to an Ivy-League physicist working on his doctorate about what he did with these verses. I loved his response:

"I feel as though, when I think about something carefully, skeptically when necessary, I am using 'the mind of Christ,' and do, when appropriate, stand behind the conclusions I reach. In short, I am reaching for His understanding when I seek hard after something, and not my own (directing my path, as verse 6 puts it)."[1]

That's about as clean and clear as it gets. I don't think you can draw these kinds of conclusions by just adopting some random philosophical stance. A person who has tapped into the relational nature of God moves from mere knowledge of Him, to the fulfillment of what Solomon is suggesting.

We *trust with all our hearts!* This is not a reckless and blind boldness, but a confident security in the One to whom we submit. This trust is backed by the impulses of our heart.

The Hebrew word for *"heart"* is **lêb** (which is pronounced *labe)*. It is widely used to convey the mind, the will and the emotions in man. There isn't too much that happens in our lives where at least one of those three isn't involved.

The final part of the text, *"in all your ways acknowledge Him,"* tells me that all those imaginary lines we use to parcel and subdivide our lives are absolved. No longer can we separate public from private, spiritual from secular, internal from external.

There are plenty of ways to acknowledge Him! But it all starts with trust!

In The Pages

Read Isaiah 45:11-13 and journal some of the highlights that jump out at you in those few verses. How do they confirm points made in today's lesson? Pray today for the *"mind of Christ"* (See Philippians 2:5-8 for tangible clues).

Shine

February 4
Proverbs 4

"But the path of the just is as the shining light, that shineth more and more unto the perfect day." Proverbs 4:18, KJV

For the second day, we entertain a passage that refers to our *paths*. We have to consider this because people in the western world don't walk anywhere anymore, unless it's for recreational purposes. We forget that less than ten percent of the world's population owns a car. There are a lot of people hoofing it out there!

I doubt Solomon walked anywhere either, but he knew that just about everyone else in the world had a great appreciation for smooth and clear paths, especially when traveling at night. I suspect that people maneuvered throughout the land on memorized footpaths and treacherous roads.

You were lucky if you had a bright moon and a torch would only stay lit for so long. So you were facing some tricky obstacles, slithery critters and all kinds of stealthy varmints out there.

In today's world, we are nervous just walking our driveways in the dark. Imagine what they faced back in the day!

Wisdom is promising an escalating progression of light for the path of the just. The **ôrach** (pronounced *o´-rakh)*, the well-trodden road, is actually maintained by God himself. A prophet weighs in:

"The way of the righteous is smooth; O Upright One, make the path of the righteous level" (Isaiah 26:7, NASB).

Clear and illuminated paths at least allow for a certain amount of security and safety. The further along we walk these righteous paths, the more illumination we get. The more illumination we get, the more confidence we gain in God's goodness!

Not only is the path being continuously brightened, but we are becoming light ourselves. What an amazing thought!

Jesus said,

"You are the light of the world. A city set on a hill cannot be hidden; nor does anyone light a lamp and put it under a basket, but on the lamp-stand, and it gives

light to all who are in the house. Let your light shine before men in such a way that they may see your good works, and glorify your Father who is in heaven" (Matthew 5:14-16, NASB).

What a vote of confidence from our Lord! It buckles my knees a bit to think that He has that much hope in us; that we are the plan upon which He wagered the cross... His suffering.

THE ADVANCEMENT OF THE KINGDOM HINGES UPON OUR WILLINGNESS TO BE THE CARRIERS OF HIS LIGHT!

Paul also brought an amazing insight to the church at Philippi:

"Do all things without grumbling or disputing; so that you will prove yourselves to be blameless and innocent, children of God above reproach in the midst of a crooked and perverse generation, among whom you appear as lights in the world" (Philippians 2:14-15, NASB).

So here it is, an opportunity to walk in His light - to become light, be light and shed abroad the light of our King! That might require a change in some of our attitudes. Right?

In The Pages

Take a look at Ephesians 5:6-14. Record your thoughts on the "highlights" of that passage. Let's shine today! SHINE!

Casting Bait

February 5
Proverbs 5

"So, my friend, listen closely; don't treat my words casually. Keep your distance from such a woman; absolutely stay out of her neighborhood." Proverbs 5:7-8, MSG

So here we are again in Proverbs 5 and there just isn't a whole lot of good news in this chapter. Other than about three verses (18-20), most everything in this chapter is a plea to avoid the pitfalls of lust, adultery and the lure of the prostitute.

I like the fact that Peterson translates the warning as, *"absolutely stay out of her neighborhood."* You need to look at a few other translations in order to understand the *why* of that statement.

The reason is simple: the prostitute is running a business. She (*BTW... I do realize all this stuff is NOT gender specific*) doesn't love her tricks. Like hawkers at a carnival, she sits in her doorway and calls out to all those passing by. Baiting them. Enticing them. This is a very obvious tactic.

People looking to pay for sexual favors know where to find such places. Whether in the red light district or just the shady side of town, water seeks its own level and like-spirits attract. Darkness knows where and how to find darkness.

In that neighborhood, the one we're told to avoid, there is a whole lot of fishing going on. They cast their lines in hopes that some aggressive sport fish or a bottom-sucker will take the bait.

Let me just say this piece and be done with it: this stuff goes on in the church also. Yeah, maybe even your church.

There are plenty of church people who are hurting, disappointed with unfulfilled expectations in their covenant relationships. Nasty situations develop in sacred places, not just on the other side of the tracks. So let's not get too self-righteous here.

Wisdom says, *"keep your distance from such a woman"* or player. While this is good, practical advice, there is something else I want us to consider.

Who is the real problem here, the prostitute or the one employing the prostitute? God genuinely loves all these people. Jesus loved these people. He didn't come to condemn them, but to save them (John 3:17). But, if there wasn't a market for sex trafficking, there would be no sex trafficking.

The heart of this whole chapter is to remind men and women that their covenant partner is the best thing God has ever given them!

If you take the bait of these ancient un-doings, you invite the very presence of hell into your life! Can we really condemn the one who cast the bait? We do NOT have to fish in these waters. We do NOT have to bite. We do NOT have to swallow the hook.

The warning to keep your distance is a good warning! The alcoholic doesn't need to work at the liquor store. He should know better.

The people struggling with lust don't need to frequent topless bars or watch porn.

They know better.

And the diabetic doesn't need to wheel into *Krispy Kreme* every day. They know better!

Likewise, if you're in a covenant relationship, you need to keep all aspects of intimacy before your mate. That includes your needs, your desires and all your longings for shared depth and relationship.

God has given us our mates for those things. To look elsewhere to fulfill any of those needs, hetero or not, is to swim in waters that are brimming with the bait of consequence.

We know better! If you take this bait, you will feel the steel.

In The Pages

"Don't treat my words casually." How would we do that? What are the dangers of being guilty of not paying attention to wisdom's teaching here? What strategy would you suggest in laying down a good and alert posture about these things?

Asleep

February 6
Proverbs 6

"But you, lazybones, how long will you sleep? When will you wake up? A little extra sleep, a little more slumber, a little folding of the hands to rest - then poverty will pounce on you like a bandit; scarcity will attack you like an armed robber." Proverbs 6:9-11, NLT

I love this version of this passage. We all identify with this simple truth, but I have a thread I want us to pursue today that really confirms a message I believe Kingdom people need to hear.

To read Solomon, it would be easy to see *poverty* as an isolated event that happens because of a mistake—maybe a period of slothfulness or not paying attention to details. My personal conviction is that poverty is a spirit.

IT CAN SO INFECT US THAT WE BECOME SUBJECTS OF POVERTY AND SCARCITY!

It begins to infiltrate and consume everything in our lives. Likewise, "scarcity" is also a spirit. We become scarcity and, if we don't fight with everything inside of us to go against that tide, we get swept up in a world of lack, clutching and protecting what little we've got left.

Then the entire focus of our lives becomes getting more than what we had yesterday, just trying to get by, and it's all up to me to make it happen!

Solomon's subjects knew about poverty. They also knew that getting behind at harvest time or planting time had serious consequences. Winter was about the only time to catch a breather.

From Solomon's time moving forward about 850 years, I want us to see another way we have to overcome our sleepiness, challenge the spirits of scarcity and poverty and walk in the full provision of faith.

The saints in Jerusalem were hurting badly. Rome was bringing the heat, a famine had plagued the agrarian culture and the need for true benevolence was manifest everywhere. In an effort to ease some of the suffering, the Apostle Paul had written a letter to the church in Corinth asking them to take up a gift offering for relief that he would personally deliver to Pastor James (1 Corinthians 16:1-9).

One year later, for whatever reason, the church in Corinth had still not taken up that offering (2 Corinthians 8:10-11). A simple reading of the text indicates Paul's disappointment.

Why hadn't they responded to the needs of their brothers and sisters in Jerusalem? Paul's dashed hopes led him to challenge their "scarcity" mindsets with a tactic we can all find most inspiring.

Paul didn't want to have to command them to take up an offering. He wanted them to be genuinely moved in their hearts and to respond to the need. Paul doesn't shame the church in Corinth; instead he lays before them the example of the churches in Macedonia:

"Now, brethren, we wish to make known to you the grace of God which has been given in the churches of Macedonia" (2 Corinthians 8:1, NASB).

THE MACEDONIAN CHURCHES WERE VERY POOR, DIRT POOR IN FACT, BUT THE SPIRIT OF POVERTY DID NOT RULE OVER THEM!

Actually, the opposite happened:

"...that in a great ordeal of affliction their abundance of joy and their deep

poverty overflowed **in the wealth of their liberality**. *For I testify that according to their ability, and beyond their ability, they gave of their own accord, begging us with much urging for the favor of participation in the support of the saints"* (2 Corinthians 8:2-4, NASB).

The Macedonian churches attacked their own lack with generosity towards another need, not with tight-fisted slothfulness and scarcity. What an amazing message of faith and courage!

We have MUCH to learn from them!

In The Pages

How closely did you examine all the scriptures in today's devo? Look at them again and record what you hear the Holy Spirit saying to you. It might be good to soak in this lesson a little longer than normal.

Boisterlicious?

February 7
Proverbs 7

"She is boisterous and rebellious, her feet do not remain at home; she is now in the streets, now in the squares, and lurks by every corner" Proverbs 7:11-12, NASB

"Brazen and brash she was, restless and roaming, never at home, walking the streets, loitering in the mall, hanging out at every corner in town." Proverbs 7:11-12, MSG

"She is unruly and defiant, her feet never stay at home; now in the street, now in the squares, at every corner she lurks." Proverbs 7:11-12, NIV

You just know that something is not right with her. Her way is not normal. It is not beautiful—it is not charming. And depending on your personal preference, it could be classified as downright offensive.

The Hebrew word for *"boisterous"* is only used four times in the Old Testament: twice in Proverbs and twice elsewhere. It's not a pleasant word. It's irksome.

In the original language of the text, **hâmâh** (pronounced *haw-maw'*) literally means, *"to make a loud sound."* But the implication is *to be in a great commotion, tumult, to rage, to moan, to be at war with everyone and everything!*

I wish—I'm sure we all wish—that this personality trait was restricted just to the male or female adulterer. But it's not. {sigh}

It is hard enough to think in terms of this life projection from a man, but when it comes off of a woman it seems to be more noticeable, more "out there," more depleted of grace.

Maybe it's the southern man in me, but when this current of wind blows from a guy, I just chalk-it-up to another "wind bag." But when a woman turns heads in a bad way I immediately think:

"What in the world has happened to this dear woman?"

It's one thing to be playfully loud and aggressive; it is quite another thing to be carrying a controlling spirit that is rooted in rejection and bitterness that produces such a caustic chemistry. Obviously, that internal restlessness has her out *there* when she should be peacefully in *here*. It is not good.

Hosea, the clean prince, had his hands full. We really do not know the whole story with Gomer. We have to fill in quite a few gaps by mere inference.

Her name means *"completion* or *fulfillment."* We know that Hosea's marriage to a known harlot was a tangible allegory to Israel's wanderings from their God. Even though Jehovah loved and chose his beloved children, they continually wandered off on idolatrous tangents that betrayed covenant.

Even after taking vows with Hosea, Gomer went back to her old ways and her old life. The most startling of instructions to Hosea were for him to go get her again. And not just to go get her, but to actually *love* her again (Hosea 3:1).

These simple instructions to a man of God in regards to his rebellious wife confirmed God's intent and willingness to forgive all and "complete" His love for Israel. I wonder if the readjustment of a woman's spirit who is now overtly aggressive and brazen has much to do with her willingness to be loved again, rescued again, sought after and fought for (one more time)?

The righteous pursuit of a willing man could possibly do the trick, but more than likely only the healing touch from the Lord can calm such rigors and bring the completion she so desperately needs. Again, the fix is in *here*, and not out *there*.

In The Pages

Dear lady, how in touch are you with your aggression levels? How open are you to the real truth about how your life projects? Who do you trust to tell you if you need to readjust your temperament and ways?

Guys, if you are married, what are you doing to offer security and internal rest for your gal? You have to meet her aggressions with some real love! Are you helping matters or do you continue to be a big source of irritation to her disappointment?

I still feel okay with this devo because of the foundational text in Proverbs that more or less highlights these problems. But, instead of re-writing the devo, let me add these few thoughts: It could be that the "boisterous" woman is the way she is, not because it's her nature, but because she's been totally wounded, disrespected, abused, and or improperly handled by men in general, and/or by her mate. The recent exposure of sexual harassment among our nation's elite and powerful does indicate that there are women who have every right to be pissed and very vocal about what they've had to endure. Not all men are pigs, but some are. Not all women are willing to take their share of abuse in order to get what they want, but some do. There really are victims out there. Maybe we've totally lost the plot and forgotten our boundaries about respecting the image of God in both male and female? It could be that everyone needs to get back to a genuine moral compass of decency that respects and values every single person? Think about it. It couldn't hurt... right? —MDP 2018

RYR Fail

February 8
Proverbs 8

"My benefits are worth more than a big salary, even a very big salary; the returns on me exceed any imaginable bonus." Proverbs 8:19, MSG

"My fruit is better than gold, yes, than fine gold, and my revenue than choice silver." Proverbs 8:19, NKJV

Timing is everything! We so desperately want a word from God, but more often than not, we are not ready to hear that word.

Earlier this morning, I was reading through some material that often feeds my soul and Richard Rohr mentioned that one of our frustrations in hearing from the Lord is that we're not asking the right questions. He states, *"The world is asking how I can be making $40,000 by the time I'm forty? Our world is completely* *obsessed with that question."* [6]

He goes on to point out that in the Gospels, Jesus continually reminds us that all of those kinds of things are passing away. Our material concerns do NOT bear eternal significance! Solomon confirms this notion.

He reminds us that the benefits of wisdom exceed all earthly riches. Really, if we sought after our connection with God and pursued wisdom as aggressively as we pursue monetary gain, it just might curb our stress and anxiety levels and produce a whole different set of questions while we sit in the presence of the Lord.

> *"And someone came to Him and said, 'Teacher, what good thing shall I do that I may obtain eternal life?' "* (Matthew 19:16, NASB)

At first glance, it appears to be a good question. But the young man, who also happened to be rich (we will refer to him as RYR for "rich young ruler"), was looking for that "good thing" he could do to tip the scales in his favor with God. So Jesus used the RYR's own paradigm to reveal what was in his heart.

Jesus presented a list of some things in the Law (murder, adultery, theft, lying, honoring parents, loving neighbors, etc.), to whet the RYR's appetite. RYR quickly confirmed his complete compliance with the externals of the Law (Matthew 19:20).

Then Jesus brought the hammer: *"If you wish to be complete, go and sell your possessions and give to the poor, and you will have treasure in heaven; and come, follow Me"* (Matthew 19:21, NASB).

In a single moment, every source of comfort and security for the RYR became the very objects that were blocking his path to knowing he had "eternal life". Jesus used the RYR's "external things" to reveal the more important conditions inside of his heart. It's a troubling encounter even now.

This is not a "your stuff is bad" message. It's also not a "give all your shit away and move to Africa" talk either.

It's a reminder from both Wisdom and the Lord Himself that the MOST valuable things in our lives have absolutely nothing to do with our money, possessions or things.

Wisdom is valuable. Relationships are precious. Forgiveness is silver. Grace is gold. Love is priceless.

In The Pages

Read Matthew 19:23-26. What lessons can you draw from these few verses? What are the questions formulating in your spirit?

Born Again... not the end!

February 9
Proverbs 9

"Give instruction to a wise man and he will be still wiser, teach a righteous man and he will increase his learning." Proverbs 9:9, NASB

I call them "Bapt-tee-costals." Good evangelicals who begin to realize there is more to living for God than just reading their Bibles and getting to church and Sunday school every week. There is no condemnation here, just an honest historical observation.

These are the spiritual rascals who begin to "sample" the gifts of the Spirit and perhaps entertain the idea that maybe, just maybe, God might still be doing miracles, signs and wonders today. They may even be willing to consider the possibility that speaking in tongues is of God and NOT of the devil.

Commonly, they huddle in small groups inside of traditional churches, usually covert, praying and believing together for a move from God that will release the presence of His Spirit and totally transform their churches and communities. The more inquisitive ones will even begin to sniff this "new wine" and maybe dip their toes into the vat to check the temperature.

And if they continue on such a course, there will always be that possibility that they will eventually fall (or jump) into that vat and become full-fledged "Chrizz-ma-tics" (gross misspelling intended). This is sort of how it has happened . . . millions of times.

I love His question:

> *"Are you the teacher of Israel and do not understand these things?"*
> (John 3:10, NASB).

Nicodemus, a respected ruler of the Pharisees, came to Jesus in secrecy because his head and heart were in conflict with one another. His heart told him that Jesus was the "real deal" and obviously authorized by heaven.

But his head knew that to be continually drafted into the wake of Jesus' way was to risk everything, including his standing with the brotherhood, possibly his credentials and definitely his reputation.

I find it interesting that one of the cornerstone verses of all Christianity evolves from Jesus' conversation with this man. Bluntly, Jesus tells this wise sage that his knowledge is to no avail if he can't see beyond his fundamental religion and ritual acceptance.

A closer examination of their dialogue pretty much confirms that Jesus is inviting Nicodemus to move beyond his religious formality, and to sample the work and presence of the Spirit! Yes, Nicodemus, you must be born again of the Spirit, but then you must *walk by* the Spirit.

There is more than a wild ride to heaven at stake.

Where the Spirit of the Lord is, the wind blows! Be willing to find out where the Spirit is going. There is so much intensity in Jesus' talk with Nicodemus!

You get the feeling that Jesus must have believed, *"Here is a man that is willing to risk it all and go for it."* Maybe Nicodemus was the first "Bapt-tee-costal" after all.

I am fairly certain that a man that deep in relationship with Jesus' tribe "got the picture" during all the "whoop-ti-doo" that occurred 40 days after the Lord finally ascended. "Business as usual," for Rabbi Nicodemus, was done for.

In The Pages

What does John 19:38-42 confirm to you about Nicodemus' decisions concerning the rest of his life? He knew the apostles personally. What influence to you think they gained from Nicodemus' spiritual direction?

Raise the Roof!

February 10
Proverbs 10

"The mouth of the righteous is a fountain of life, but the mouth of the wicked conceals violence." Proverbs 10:11, NIV

My current spiritual community is into making loud and bold declarations. It's the belief that throwing truth into the spiritual realm about what we know to be true about our selves and others has a significant impact on the events and destiny for our life.

We are constantly challenging each other to speak life, NOT death!

"Words kill, words give life; they're either poison or fruit—you choose"
(Proverbs 18:21, MSG).

Prophesy (*means to speak a higher truth regardless of what circumstance is manifest*) change when it gets tough. Griping accomplishes nothing productive.

I thought today would be a great day for you to stand on your bed, your couch, a chair or a table, and let the truth fly loudly, boldly and with a great hope that your attitude and God's help will bring about the fulfillment of His plan for your life! Let's go make some declarations! Proclamations! Shout and raise the roof!

I AM FULL OF CHRIST!
I AM ANOINTED BY THE HOLY SPIRIT!
I AM GOD'S FAVORITE CHILD!
THERE IS A GREAT DESTINY FOR MY LIFE!
GOD CREATED ME FOR A REASON!
IT IS NO ACCIDENT THAT I AM HERE!
MY GIFTS ARE LEGITIMATE!
I AM UNIQUELY FASHIONED!
NO ONE ELSE IS LIKE ME!
I HAVE GENERATIONAL BLESSINGS WITH MY NAME ON THEM!
I AM BLESSED AND HIGHLY FAVORED BY THE LORD!

I AM A SPIRITUAL LIFE-GIVER!
PEOPLE GET BLESSED WHEN I AM AROUND!
I AM AN EMOTIONAL LIFE-GIVER!
I HURT WHEN OTHERS HURT!
I CARE ABOUT WHAT OTHERS CARE ABOUT!
I PREFER OTHERS ABOVE MYSELF!
I HAVE JOY WHEN OTHERS REJOICE!
I WILL CONFIRM GOD'S FAVOR ON OTHERS!
I WILL PROPHESY LIFE OVER MY FAMILY!
I WILL PROPHESY LIFE OVER MY FRIENDS!
I WILL PROPHESY LIFE OVER THE HOPELESS!
PEOPLE WILL GET WELL WHEN I PRAY FOR THEM!

PEOPLE WILL BE BLESSED WHEN I STAND
IN AGREEMENT WITH THEM!

THE KINGDOM OF GOD SHOWS UP WHEN I SHOW UP!
I CHOOSE TO BE FULL OF FAITH!
I CHOOSE TO FORGIVE OTHERS WHEN I AM WRONGED!
I WILL BLESS THE LORD, O MY SOUL!
I AM BLESSED AND HIGHLY FAVORED BY THE LORD!

I WILL BE AT PEACE!
I WILL BE AT REST!
I WILL NOT CONTROL!
I WILL TRUST IN THE LORD!
GOD SEES ALL! HE IS MY SOURCE!
HE IS MY PROVISION! HE IS MY HELP!
HE IS MY FRIEND!
THE HOLY SPIRIT HAS MY BACK!
HE IS MY COMFORT!
HE IS MY SHIELD!
HE IS MY DEFENSE!

NO WEAPON FORMED AGAINST ME WILL PROSPER!
GOD IS MY STRONG TOWER!
GOD IS MY REFUGE!
GOD IS FOR ME!
GOD LOVES ME!
GOD LIKES ME!
I AM BLESSED AND HIGHLY FAVORED BY THE LORD!

TODAY WILL BE A GREAT DAY!
TODAY, I WILL SEE GOD MOVE!
TODAY, GOOD THINGS WILL HAPPEN!
I WILL SPEAK LIFE TODAY!
I WILL SPEAK BLESSINGS TODAY!
I WILL LOVE TODAY!
I WILL LAUGH TODAY!
I WILL PRAISE GOD TODAY!
THE KINGDOM WILL COME TODAY!
HALLELUJAH!
LORD, I PRAISE YOU!

I AM BLESSED AND HIGHLY FAVORED BY THE LORD!

Multi-generational

February 11
Proverbs 11

"When a wicked man dies, his expectation will perish, and the hope of the unjust perishes." Proverbs 11:7, NKJV

I've never been much of a planner. I've usually adopted the stance of *"Let's just find out when we get there."* But honestly, the older I get the more it presses on my spirit that we need to consider how our ways today affect our future realities. Not just for myself, but for those who follow behind me.

God is all about *who* and *what* follows behind us. He is multi-generation focused! Scripture is jam-packed with references verifying God's desire for the transfer of blessing from one generation to another. Here is a good example:

"Now when Abram was ninety-nine years old, the Lord appeared to Abram and said to him, 'I am God Almighty; walk before Me, and be blameless. I will establish My covenant between Me and you, and I will multiply you exceedingly.' Abram fell on his face, and God talked with him, saying, 'As for Me, behold, My covenant is with you, and you will be the father of a multitude of nations. No longer shall your name be called Abram, but your name shall be Abraham; for I will make you the father of a multitude of nations. I have made you exceedingly fruitful, and I will make nations of you, and kings will come forth from you. I will establish My covenant between Me and you and your descendants after you throughout their generations for an everlasting covenant, to be God to you and to your descendants after you. I will give to you and to your descendants after you, the land of your sojournings, all the land of Canaan, for an everlasting possession; and I will be their God.' God said further to Abraham, 'Now as for you, you shall keep My covenant, you and your descendants after you throughout their generations'" (Genesis 17:1-9, NASB).

We cannot deny the fact that God has a great interest in us proactively stewarding what we now possess with a "what comes behind us" mentality.

Even a 16-year-old has the opportunity to put desires, actions, attitudes, disciplines and tangible blessings into motion for a prophetic hope that will release blessings for his or her soon-to-come children, grand-children and future generations!

That is a very real benefit, not to mention duty, in our spiritual pilgrimage today.

Wisdom tells us that it is a waste not to be engaged in God's overall purpose for our existence. To only be concerned with what is in front of our faces this very day is selfish, small-minded, and downright missing the mark.

We forfeit one of the greatest privileges of following God when we cannot get beyond our own self-centeredness! God has great plans for the generations that follow us! We are invited to play a part in their blessing!

I suspect that men and women who only live for themselves do leave some sort of vapor trail, but I'm not so sure it always translates into a big blessing for those who come after them!

Kingdom people care about leaving a great spiritual inheritance to family and loved ones. And let me tell you, there is more to inheritance than titles, land and money! Much more!

In The Pages

What kind of future gifts do you want to see bestowed upon your children and grandchildren? Ask the Lord for eyes to see what's ahead. Pray fervently for their increase!

Locks on the Inside

February 12
Proverbs 12

"In the way of righteousness is life, and in its pathway there is no death." Proverbs 12:28, NASB

"I am the door: by me if any man enter in, he shall be saved, and shall go in and out, and find pasture. The thief cometh not, but for to steal, and to kill, and to destroy: I am come that they might have life, and that they might have it more abundantly." John 10:9-10, KJV

Obviously, under the new covenant, only the blood of Jesus brings forth our righteousness. It's a faith transaction on our parts to receive (believe) the finished and absolute work of the atonement.

"He made Him who knew no sin to be sin on our behalf, so that we might become the righteousness of God in Him" (2 Corinthians 5:21, NASB).

Paul says elsewhere,

"More than that, I count all things to be loss in view of the surpassing value of knowing Christ Jesus my Lord, for whom I have suffered the loss of all things, and count them but rubbish so that I may gain Christ, and may be found in Him, not having a righteousness of my own derived from the Law, but that which is through faith in Christ, the righteousness which comes from God on the basis of faith, that I may know Him and the power of His resurrection and the fellowship of His sufferings, being conformed to His death; in order that I may attain to the resurrection from the dead" (Philippians 3:8-11, NASB).

A person fully alive and aware of the power of these truths has the opportunity to tap into that abundant life Jesus promises. But I think we ought to note that it's not a given guarantee.

We *do* have that abundant life at our disposal, BUT our choices factor into whether or not we experience the full benefits of what He has offered us.

After hanging around the sheep pen for as long as I have, I'm fairly convinced that only a small portion of the Body of Christ is really living in the fullness of that abundant life Jesus offered.

It's a dangerous world out there. Bad stuff happens to good people. Devout and loving people hurt the ones they love the most. Babies get sick. Marriages dissolve. Governments topple. Disappointment looms.

How we react to these things has plenty to do with whether or not we feel *abundantly* loved by God, or anyone else for that matter.

I've noticed that when we really get hurt, we build walls that separate us from people and things that remind us of our pain. In fact, we have gotten so good at building these walls we suddenly look up and realize we are in a prison of our own doing!

My good friend Michael Hindes specifically identifies these **5 prisons** as:

1) Comparison, 2) Regret, 3) Bitterness, 4) Excuses and **5) Withdrawal.**[7]

We are all too familiar with each of these prisons and we all should know what we have to do to get out of them. **We have to forgive.** We must release those who have hurt us and ask the Holy Spirit to renew our thoughts and paths.

As I was writing today's lesson, I believe the Lord showed me a very clear picture. The locks to the doors of these prisons are on the *inside* of the cell doors, not the outside.

Clearly, we have the keys to set ourselves free. But will we use them?

In The Pages

Which prison are you in? Why are you waiting to set yourself free? Isn't it time to get back on the path of freedom and life?

Holy Smack-Talkin'!

February 13
Proverbs 13

"Through insolence comes nothing but strife, but wisdom is with those who receive counsel." Proverbs 13:10, NASB

I believe this verse to be very true. If you approach any situation with *insolence*, you can expect a confrontation sooner or later.

The word **zâdôwn** (pronounced *zaw-done'*) means *"arrogant pride,"* which you can bet people are going to have an issue with. True arrogant pride is a nasty thing. Prideful people have problems with *over-stating* and *under-delivering*.

Wisdom tells us you can expect problems to eventually manifest wherever true insolence is involved. But here is the kicker: sometimes what appears to be arrogance is actually a God-deposited boldness. If that's the case, the Holy Spirit will confirm it.

Internal motivation is the telltale sign of whether or not something is coming from a place of insolence. If it is coming out of the wrong power source, everyone will know soon enough.

The word *"insolence"* is only used three times in the entire Old Testament: once in today's text, once in Hosea, and once in 1 Samuel with the story of David and Goliath.

David was the youngest of his father's eight sons. Scripture tells us he was definitely model material, fit for the cover of a magazine. I don't really picture a muscled-up kid though. I'm sure his chores on the slopes of Bethlehem, coupled with the tanning effects of those crisp sunny days made David look like any other southern California surfer dude.

After his anointing by Samuel, David became Saul's armor bearer, a job that required him to be in fairly close proximity to the King at all times. Undoubtedly, David had heard the King talk privately about the glory of Israel and the faithfulness of God. Such talk inspires young men.

Even if Saul had been sarcastic and flippant, David was downloading the truth in great quantities.

So when David showed up at the campsite of Israel's greatest warriors, he noticed that Israel's firepower wasn't on display. In fact, someone had hung the "out to lunch" sign in the window.

No one was willing to face the arrogant taunting of Goliath. When David asked an honest question, he un-nerved everyone!

"What will be done for the man who kills this Philistine and takes away the reproach from Israel? For who is this uncircumcised Philistine, that he should taunt the armies of the living God?" (1 Samuel 17:26, NASB).

The rebuke David received told the whole story!

Remember what I said earlier about God-given boldness and insolent pride looking almost identical on the front end?

Everyone was so frikk'n paralyzed with fear that David's question rendered an explosive response from his eldest brother, Eliab.

"Why have you come down? And with whom have you left those few sheep in the wilderness? I know your insolence and the wickedness of your heart; for you have come down in order to see the battle" (1 Samuel 17:28, NASB).

Strife *does* follow foolish arrogance, but in this case, David had God's endorsement to back up the words and the position of his heart. This time it wasn't *insolence*, but anointed boldness!

From the moment of his eldest brother's rebuke, until the removal of Goliath's head it was complete madness!

A wiry teenager scrambling for stones, talking smack, taunting the big warrior—everyone was undone! Then, with the flick of his wrist, David's stone found the sweet spot and the air of insolence was sucked right out of the atmosphere!

God had David's back (the back of holy boldness). The Book of Acts is full of such encounters! (*Acts 4:31; 9:27-28; 13:46; 14:3; 18:26; 19:8*)

In The Pages

Have you ever felt the surge of holy boldness? I have missed God's timing in the past and over-stated with insolence in my heart. The results were not so good. Can you identify? How do you read the difference in your heart?

Healing Hearts *Do* Love

February 14
Proverbs 14

"A tranquil heart is life to the body, but passion is rottenness to the bones." Proverbs 14:30, NASB

Happy *LOVE* day! Did you do something thoughtful for the one who has your heart? If not, make that happen today sooner rather than later.

It doesn't require extravagance or commercialized patronage. Whatever it is, let the expression be real. Genuine exploits of love are rare and underrated.

Sir, if you give her a card, how about a loving kiss and a warm hug before shoving that $5 singing Elvis card into her hand? In other words, leave her with more than just glitter in her hair and a small paper cut.

Dear woman, real respect and warm gestures of love can melt a man! Take advantage of the celebration and make all the intimate connections you possibly can. If your romantic juices are flowing, I'd bet BIG MONEY that man will respond! God smiles on this.

**So let the angels sing and the cherubs dance!
It's a fun day to be in love!**

This *"tranquil heart"* thing ties in perfectly today. The word for *tranquil* is **marpê**' (prounounced mar-pay') and it means, *"curative medicine, health, soundness; a healing remedy."*

People who can really rest in their "love-ability" (ease to give and receive love) are just happier and healthier people. Not that love is a cure-all, but we unleash the most amazing waves of influence in our lives when we embrace all the different strains of love – eros (sensual), philĕō (friendship) and agapē (unconditional God love).

We are most like our Creator when we are in processes of love!

He knew what we needed when He designed us. When Adam saw Eve for the first time, we can only imagine what must have crossed his mind!

There she stood, naked, designed by God to rock his world! Once Adam had finished naming all of creation, he must have realized what a genius God was, having given him someone to love who was absolutely perfect for him.
She was like nothing else he had ever seen! He was fulfilled! Rich, true, honest love heals us all!

Wisdom points out that *passion* or *jealous envy* only want for themselves. These runaway emotions don't have the capacity to really give away love. They can only protect what they already have and parcel out only that which they can control.

That is not God's kind of love. Real love is built upon trust and God set it up that way. He had to!

Having a choice to love (or not) is the only way to measure whether the love is real. Anything else is like rotten decay to our lives.

Eugene Peterson has translated Paul's classic exposition on love so beautifully. Ponder and meditate on this poetry:

"I'm bankrupt without love. Love never gives up. Love cares more for others than for self. Love doesn't want what it doesn't have. Love doesn't strut, doesn't have a swelled head, doesn't force itself on others, isn't always "me first," doesn't fly off the handle, doesn't keep score of the sins of others, doesn't revel when others grovel, takes pleasure in the flowering of truth, puts up with anything, trusts God always, always looks for the best, never looks back, but keeps going to the end" (1 Corinthians 13:3-7, MSG.)

You just know there is healing in our bones for this!

In The Pages

Okay, it's Valentine's Day! When is the last time you wrote a love letter? I figure I'm not making any friends over at Hallmark, but why not construct your own love letter to that person who needs your healing and loving words! You might find it also soothes your own soul!

Right on Time!

February 15
Proverbs 15

"A man has joy in an apt answer, and how delightful is a timely word!" Proverbs 15:23, NASB

"The Lord God has given Me the tongue of disciples, that I may know how to sustain the weary one with a word. He awakens Me morning by morning, He awakens My ear to listen as a disciple." Isaiah 50:4, NASB

When you get a real download from the Lord, it's better than 1,000 sermons! A word can flip your world upside down, especially when you understand the timing of that word. But that's the hard part.

In 1999, I decided I wanted to take my eldest daughter overseas to do some humanitarian relief work together for her high school graduation gift. We were headed to Albania to work in a refugee camp for a couple weeks.

The day I bought our non-refundable airline tickets, a prophet (yes, a real prophet guy) spoke over me that night in a home group meeting. He said, *"Mike, the direction that you are planning to go is the wrong direction. Turn around 180 degrees and go in the opposite direction! Obey, and you'll see God like never before."*

I freaked out because there was no way he could have known what I had done that day!

So I went home, found an old *National Geographic* map of the world and drew a line from Texas to Albania. Then I drew a line in the opposite direction. It passed through two places where I actually knew ministers who lived there. One place was in the Philippines. The other was Uganda.

I called the missionary I knew in the Philippines and he said he wasn't interested in our coming. He basically told me to *buzz off*. Great! That's clear and timely enough!

I made a second long-distance call to my contact in Uganda and began to tell him about how I had bought the plane tickets, about the meeting the night before and the prophetic word I had received. The whole time I was telling my story, he was laughing on the other end of the phone.

Once he gained composure, he said, *"Pastor Mike, the leaders of my church and*

I have been praying and fasting for the last three days! We asked God to deliver to us an American pastor who would come to Uganda to preach our crusade in the village of Bugiri! God has sent you!"

I was in shock. But the next day, I went back to Delta and told the woman at the desk the whole story. She said, *"You know those tickets are non-refundable, non-exchangeable?"*

I said, *"Yes, I'm afraid so."* Then, to my utter amazement, she said, *"But this time we're going to bend the rules."*

By now my head was swirling! Not only did they exchange our tickets, but our ride over the pond was in Business Class! Come on Jesus!

I would have to say that what happened in Uganda after all that commotion confirmed every word the prophet had spoken that night.

A *timely word*, a right word, an encouraging word sent us on the adventure of a lifetime! What we experienced was incredible! We saw the Lord move with unmistakable power! It was epic perfection!

The right and timely word for us!

In The Pages

What is your "truth is stranger than fiction" story about God's word? How at ease are you with God's timing? How often do you chalk things like this up to coincidence?

Redemption Rain

February 16
Proverbs 16

"In the light of [our] King's face is life, and his favor is like a cloud with the spring rain. Proverbs 16:15, NASB

I'm hung in a song right now. Jonathan and Melissa Helser have written another amazing song, this time about God's redemption rain.[8] I want to share some of the words with you. Do yourself a favor today and download the entire album. *Redemptive Rain* is still falling. Get out and play in the rain!

REDEMPTION RAIN
Used by Permission

Won't you come up here? Come up high.
Won't you sing His praise? Let it rise.
Up from your ashes and all your pain.
Won't you come and dance in redemption's rain.
Come up here!
Redemption rain is falling down, down, down
Redemption's love is pouring out, out , out
Redemption's song is singing love, love, love
He is singing love, love, love
He is singing love, love, love

Won't you come up here? Come up now.
Won't you leave your worries below the clouds.
And let His beauty fill your lungs.
The heavenly chorus has begun.
Come up here!

Redemption rain is falling down, down, down
Redemption's love is pouring out, out, out
Redemption's song is singing love, love, love
He is singing love, love, love
He is singing love, love, love

Love be in my bones, love shake down my walls
Love be in my bones, love shake down my walls
Love be in my bones, love shake down my wall

In The Pages

What was it like when you first felt the refreshing rain of redemption? How did it affect you as a person? What changed in your life once you "knew" what you had never known?

Crazies

February 17
Proverbs 17

"Grandchildren are the crowning glory of the aged; parents are the pride of their children." Proverbs 17:6, NLT

"Grandchildren are like a crown to the elderly, and the glory of children is their parents." Proverbs 17:6, NET

No kidding. I used to think there was something wrong with people who made such a fuss about their grandchildren. I just didn't get it.

When I would hear of people selling their homes, picking up and moving to wherever their kids were, all because of the arrival of a new grandbaby, I'd just roll my eyes and think, *"Frikk'n losers!"*

I mean, digital pictures are just as good as being there, right?

Then in 2008, Patti and I found out that our youngest daughter (who lived 850 miles away) was pregnant with twins! We lost our minds!

We did okay with the distance up until about a month before she was due. After that, we realized that trying to keep Nana in Texas while those babies were in Colorado was just not going to work. So we transitioned, slowly, painfully, but absolutely - because we were in love!

I still can't really wrap my mind around it. How could 12 pounds of newborn twins be powerful enough to get us to uproot our entire lives?

We were sensible people, intelligent, fairly young and healthy. People like us don't do things like that, do they?

But when I held those babies for the first time, looked into their eyes and prophesied over their spirits, all I could do was weep. They demanded nothing, yet they pulled on reservoirs of love that I didn't even know existed in me.

It absolutely and completely sealed our lunacy!

There is a great give-n-take in parenting. In a perfect world, the parents provide, meet needs, develop character and offer all kinds of love (unconditional, conditional, and tough when necessary). Then, we get to enjoy the first fruits of watching our kids grow and mature. It's awesome!

In return, our children begin to understand as they get older just how much their parents helped influence and sustain them through childhood. Our front-row seat into each other's lives pretty much exposes the strengths and weakness of all parties involved.

It surely did in my life. Honestly, I think I developed more as a person than my kids while they were growing up.

But the rules are different for grandparents. We love—and that's about it.

I have the greatest memories of all my grandparents. I can't imagine being more confirmed or loved by any of them! They carried out their roles well and now it's my turn to do mine!

And before you know it, it will be your turn to do yours.

It's a great work! You'll love joining the ranks of the other crazies out there!

In The Pages

Why not write today how thankful you are for your grandparents. What did they do for you that no one else did? What are some of your favorite memories? How did they impact your life?

What Did You Say?

February 18
Proverbs 18

"He who answers a matter before he hears it, it is folly and shame to him." Proverbs 18:13, NKJV

I'm going to air out some dirty laundry today. But first let me lay down a disclaimer: this is an issue in my life I am still working on.

Although I can look back on my childhood, remember how my family gets when we're excited, and pinpoint precisely why this is such a problem for me, the responsibility is squarely upon my shoulders now. I know better and my loving wife helps keep me in check.

I'm referring to the nasty habit of talking over another person when they're trying to make a point, or even just sharing information. If I don't make a conscious effort, I'll cut you off in a heartbeat with my own grand exposition.

And I see this as a growing trend in today's world. We all think we have so much to say and contribute.

Over the years, I've noticed how my family communicates. It's not at all uncommon for everyone in the house to talk at the same time. And if we think no one is listening, we just talk louder!

Although quite comical, it can be extremely frustrating at times. It's hard to get through a simple phone call sometimes without wanting to rip the phone cord out of the wall. It's our way, but it's not too effective. As I said, I'm working on it.

Part of the problem is the **"me-monster"** effect. When that bad boy begins to manifest, people get offended. How is it that we don't have time for one another anymore?

We have all this technology and means of communication at our fingertips and somehow our communication is getting worse. In fact, it may actually be inflating the problem.

My wife recently expressed her feelings about people who *NEVER* respond to phone messages, emails, texts or any other attempt to be reached for communication: *"It's rude! Downright rude!"*

She also expressed that we shouldn't be controlled by any of these sources of communication, but if you have made yourself accessible, then you should at least make attempts to respond. If you are not going to respond, then don't make yourselves accessible.

It's like being in your house and a friend or family member dropping by to check on you. They ring the doorbell, but you don't answer because you can't be inconvenienced. All the while, your guest is still standing on your front porch and knows very well that you are home.

My wife is probably right. It is *"downright rude."*

Granted, not everything that pulls at us is priority, and that includes people and their drama. We should have the right to call a time-out when we're on overload or need to establish boundaries.

Or, it could be that we have packed our lives full of so much other "activity" that we don't think we can spare time for those we really love.

 Maybe it's about time we stop and think about what kind of messages we are sending. Maybe, we need to kill the **"me-monster"** and genuinely get interested in another person's life.

Solomon offers some sound words here. One of the side notes in the NET Bible mentions that the "Mishnah" (the oral traditions of the Law) taught that a person who will not listen, over talks in communication, over states facts and impatiently cuts off another person's dialogue with his or her own responses, gives evidence to a lack of manners and culture.

Wisdom says, "It is *shameful,"* and yes Ms. Patti, it is rude! It definitely sends the message that we are too engrossed in our own ideas. We need to do better.

As I said, I'm working on it!

In The Pages

Let's be honest here. How are you doing with this topic? Have you ever felt that you were not being listened to? How did that make you feel about your importance to that person? What thoughts did you have about their methods?

Brutal Truth

February 19
Proverbs 19

"All the brothers of a poor man hate him; how much more do his friends abandon him! He pursues them with words, but they are gone." Proverbs 19:7, NASB

Sometimes the transparency of Wisdom is frikk'n uncomfortable. Whether something is right or wrong morally isn't always the point. The fact that a truth has been revealed so bluntly, without apology, is what we're not used to.

Sometimes I liken it to watching the Nature Channel. The way animals are with one another sometimes is just naturally brutal, especially when it comes to the "selection processes," or how they handle the weak, or why some critters get "Alpha" status.

We've all heard the phrase, "Tigers eat their young." It's not because they're hungry. It's all about weeding out the weak, spreading the strongest DNA, keeping the group alive and staying strong.

We cringe at the thought of an adult tiger killing poor, defenseless kittens. But the females won't ovulate while they're nursing babies. And if he's earned a spot as "head honcho," he handles it.

Within days of losing her cubs, the female is ready to mate again and even becomes the aggressor in the process. See, right or wrong isn't the issue. It's just the way it naturally works in that domain.

So I suspect what Solomon is saying here is meant to motivate our younger generations to pursue industriousness. He is making the point that laziness and irresponsibility have serious drawbacks. Point taken.

I'm not exactly sure what all is implied by *"down on your luck,"* but the general consensus in our culture is that, if you're in financial need, you've been irresponsible, stupid or you're just lazy. Sometimes that is the absolute truth... but not always.

I remember a time when I had acquired some credit card debt that put me under tremendous pressure for a season. The situation wasn't because of irresponsibility or laziness.

I was a student, serving a church, going to Seminary, with a wife and two babies, living off a pauper's wages. People on welfare were making more money than me.

Many years later, some of that stuff still reflected on my credit. When I turned in an application to rent a house, the realtor saw my credit score and said, *"Mike, you have a college degree! How could you have let that happen?"* The assumption was that I had been stupid.

Maybe I had. Most people think that way, thus the bluntness of today's proverb.

Maybe we should all be a little more sensitive to those in need around us. Before we judge them, maybe we should try to learn the whole story.

If it is indeed irresponsibility, maybe they were never really taught about stewardship. Perhaps you could be the friend, the parent or the mentor they never had.

I'm not suggesting you bail them out. I'm saying be their friend. Based on what Wisdom is laying down here, they could probably use a friend right about now.

In The Pages

When you hear the word "bankruptcy," what is your reaction? Do you have friends who struggle financially? Do you have an opinion about their plight, or do you have real insight and know their story? How have you tried to help them?

Pure?

February 20
Proverbs 20

"Who can say, I have made my heart clean, I am pure from my sin?" Proverbs 20:9, KJV

"Therefore do not go on passing judgment before the time, but wait until the Lord comes who will both bring to light the things hidden in the darkness and disclose the motives of men's hearts; and then each man's praise will come to him from God." 1 Corinthians 4:5, NASB

One of the greatest benefits of living in the New Covenant established by Christ's death on the cross is that we don't have to live under the tremendous pressure of having to get everything right in our lives, specifically, in accordance with the terms of the Old Covenant.

Sin isn't excused, overlooked or liberally allowed without negative consequence, but we have the opportunity to live in the full pardon and righteous power of our Deliverer.

We are cleansed and reconciled to God only by His blood. It is a fundamental doctrine of Christianity. We sin when we choose to sin. Our attitude is sour when we allow it to be sour. Our motives are wrong when we move towards self-serving goals at another person's expense.

Solomon was obviously operating under the old covenant, but the point is still well taken: we need something else other than our own confession to make us clean—some "thing" (some "ONE") bigger, divinely righteous, and supernaturally pure.

Can we also appreciate Paul's sensitive reminder not to make assumptions about what is going on in another person's heart?

Most of the references to *"motives"* regarding man's heart have negative overtones in scripture. Our problem is that we do all kinds of things in our religious or spiritual cultures today for the wrong reasons.

Just because it looks right, doesn't mean it is right.

God sees motives. He knows the desires of our hearts. He knows if selfish ambition or pride is involved.

As Paul says, "***HE*** *will bring to light the things hidden."* It is not our job to monitor people's motivations. We don't see the whole picture.

"Now I want you to know, brethren, that my circumstances have turned out for the greater progress of the gospel, so that my imprisonment in the cause of Christ has become well known throughout the whole praetorian guard and to everyone else, and that most of the brethren, trusting in the Lord because of my imprisonment, have far more courage to speak the word of God without fear. Some, to be sure, are preaching Christ even from envy and strife, but some also from good will; the latter do it out of love, knowing that I am appointed for the defense of the gospel; the former proclaim Christ out of selfish ambition rather than from pure motives, thinking to cause me distress in my imprisonment. What then? Only that in every way, whether in pretense or in truth, Christ is proclaimed; and in this I rejoice" (Philippians 1:12-18, NASB).

What Paul is showing us is that, while some people may preach the gospel with the intention of proclaiming Christ and advancing the Kingdom, others may preach the gospel out of selfish ambition.

Our job is not to judge the motive behind other people's actions, but to be responsible for our own motives and to do everything out of love. Paul rejoiced in the fact that Christ was promoted, whatever the motivation!

What the devil intends for evil, God can use for good. But who wants to be guilty of doing the right thing for the wrong reason?

The One we serve is living and relational. Motive and righteous purpose is important!

In The Pages

How open are you to God's voice concerning the real motives of your heart? Do you fear the truth from Him? Do you totally trust your heart?

Futility

February 21
Proverbs 21

"There is no wisdom and no understanding and no counsel against the Lord."
Proverbs 21:30, NASB

The thing that was so grating about Joseph's story was that his father and brothers knew what his dream meant. They knew it was from God, and there wasn't a frikk'n thing they could do about it. And yet, the brothers still tried (Genesis 37).

It's ok to be really upset with the Lord. He will not smite you for being angry with Him. God is strong enough to handle your emotional diatribe. But despite our objections, confusion, or anger, sooner or later we have to deal with the fact that He is God, and we are not.

That's pretty much the way the story goes. Sometimes we get answers, and sometimes we do not. And the sooner we can have peace about that, the better.

It is a startling revelation to find out that the Apostle Peter, the original Rock, the one who had so much intimate contact with Jesus, would have to stand before other Jewish believers to defend his actions.

In Acts 11 Peter recounts the rendezvous he had with some hungry Gentiles in Cornelius' home. Remember how the Holy Spirit had gone to great lengths to get the message to Peter that the gospel was no longer restricted to just his Jewish brothers and sisters?

The Holy Spirit gave him a vision that offended his mind, yet it confirmed that the Gentiles were also welcome into Jesus' fold. So Peter went with Cornelius' servants and arrived at a packed house in Caesarea to deliver what he now understood to be the "new" truth.

Upon hearing the revelation, the men and women in Cornelius' home received the Lord and a fresh baptism by the Holy Spirit was poured out:

"While Peter was still speaking these words, the Holy Spirit fell upon all those who were listening to the message. All the circumcised believers who came with Peter were amazed, because the gift of the Holy Spirit had been poured out on the Gentiles also. For they were hearing them speaking with tongues and exalting God" (Acts 10:44-46, NASB).

It was a "world changing" event!
One of the biggest since Christ's resurrection!

Had that day not happened, you and I would most likely still be peering in from the outer courts as observers... not participants.

It didn't take long for the news to get out. And *boy*, did the established Jewish (circumcised) believers take up issue with Peter.

I've often heard that the greatest resistance to a new wave coming to shore is the old wave retreating back into the ocean. Unfortunately, this is also very true in our spiritual communities.

Peter recalled: *"And as I began to speak, the Holy Spirit fell upon them just as He did upon us at the beginning. And I remembered the word of the Lord, how He used to say, 'John baptized with water, but you will be baptized with the Holy Spirit.' Therefore if God gave to them the same gift as He gave to us also after believing in the Lord Jesus Christ, who was I that I could stand in God's way?"* (Acts 11:15-17, NASB).

It was a serious question! Who in the heck am I to stand in the way of what God wants to do?

The Spirit fell on those Gentiles just like He fell upon converted Jews on the day of Pentecost. That was God's doing, not man's. God gave those gifts! Why would anyone try to interfere with what God is doing?

He is going to do what He wants to do, like it or not! Obstruction in regards to the work of the Holy Spirit is a bad idea... every time.

In The Pages

What aversion do you have to how God works? Do you only give permission to the Holy Spirit to work within the confines of your theology? Are you open to God coloring outside the lines of your normal religious experience? Be honest.

Lions, Tigers, and Bears, Oh My!

February 22
Proverbs 22

"The lazy person says, "There is a lion outside! I shall be killed in the streets!" Proverbs 22:13, NRSV

Punk'd! There is no lion. There never was a lion. It is just an excuse. I once heard a quote from Charles Swindoll that defined an "excuse" as: *a lie wrapped in the skin of rationalization.*

When I was about 10 years old, I removed the spark plug from the lawn mower on a hot summer day, attempted to crank it about three times and then proceeded to call my dad and tell him that the grass-eater was broke. *"Sorry Dad, I won't be able to mow the lawn today."*

Dad was home in 15 minutes, the mower was running within another five and my little stunt had earned me a bonus punishment on top of still having to mow the lawn. Oh, the energy we expel when we are wrapped up in our own excuses.

Not everyone really wants to get free.

The years we've spent in personal discipleship and church ministry have taught Patti and I that simple truth. Some people like the idea of freedom, but aren't willing to confront the hard issues in their lives in order to be delivered out of their bondage.

Our prisons of excuses and blame provide excellent cover, preventing us from ever getting any real help.

If you have a nasty habit or a behavioral flaw, I bet you've probably got quite the list of excuses why you can't seem to conquer that behavior. Some of those reasons may very well be legitimate and the source of your wounds, but until we are willing to push past those excuses and enter into God's grace and forgiveness, we'll be stuck in a prison of our own making and at a spiritual plateau.

We get so caught up in our past, it just seems easier to make excuses rather than progress. You might be sitting there right now, trying to rationalize how your situation is different, all the while making excuses and justifying negative behaviors:

"Lions and tigers and bears... oh my! I'll be eaten alive if I go out there!"

I know how this works. We think, *"You have no idea what I've been through!"* Or we say, *"What happened to me is **un-for-give-a-ble**!"* Trust me, I get it.

Again, this is not a *"just-get-over-it"* message. What I am proposing to you is that **HE gets it**. Nothing has ever happened to you that He doesn't know about!

That, in and of itself, may totally piss you off. HE is not put off by your anger towards him. Like it or not, believe it or not, feel it or not, **GOD LOVES YOU**.

Be reminded of Paul's words,

"And you were dead in your trespasses and sins, in which you formerly walked according to the course of this world" (Ephesians 6:1-2, NASB).

He also said,

"But where sin abounded, grace abounded much more" (Romans 5:20, NKJV).

Even on our meanest, darkest, dirtiest, ugliest, and most corrupt days, Jesus still offers us His grace and forgiveness! He can and will help us forgive what we have been unable to forgive in our wounded state. This is how we get out of our prisons.

In The Pages

Are there any excuses you've partnered with that hold your heart captive from freedom? What sin was committed towards you that God will not or cannot forgive? How does Romans 5:20 respond to that last question?

Feeding Rejection

February 23
Proverbs 23

"Do not join those who drink too much wine or gorge themselves on meat, for drunkards and gluttons become poor, and drowsiness clothes them in rags." Proverbs 23:20-21, NIV

The whole western world can't have a thyroid problem, can it? Isn't that our excuse for our struggle with obesity? Sure, maybe it's an accurate diagnosis in some cases, but what about the rest of us?

The abuse of *anything* (food, drugs, alcohol, sex, children, people, animals or pretty much anything you want to insert here... including yourself) points to deeper issues.

No one wakes up one day and decides to be a drunk. People don't decide at age fourteen to weigh 400 lbs by their fortieth birthday. No one comes out of the womb with a predetermined disposition to become a heroin addict, a fireman, tattoo artist or a missionary.

Stuff happens in our lives that influence the choices we make. We decide as we go (okay, some stuff gets decided for us). Our circumstances and how we choose to handle those circumstances, has almost everything to do with how well we cope with the good and bad things life throws at us.

I'm a mystic, so I also believe in spiritual influences. I believe that dark forces use machetes of evil that blaze trails into dense jungles of peril and darkness. And if we allow it, we follow those influences down those trails.

We can get lost in there. And what we are left with is the choice to either cope or medicate. Honestly, I don't think we're doing too well with the whole "covering up our pain" thing.

ANGRY RELIGIOUS RULES AND PRESSURE ONLY MAKE MATTERS WORSE!

Too often it seems that's all our religious systems offer is: rules and pressure. I don't think it's helping anyone.

Wisdom is always trying to get us to see below the surface. It isn't our job to judge people. My role, your role, is to manifest enough love so we become a safe place where people can take a look at what is really going on inside of their lives.

After a nice hot shower, I can go to the mirror and see that I am about 25 lbs heavier than I was while in college. I'm a Physical Ed major, for heaven's sake! I know better!

It could be that my metabolism has slowed down after 55 years and I just need to cut back, watch the sweets and exercise with more vengeance. It would not be okay for me to gorge myself because I'm bored, depressed or coming into agreement with a deep dislike of myself.

ADDICTIVE COMPULSIVE PERSONALITIES USUALLY KEEP A STEADY STREAM OF "FEEL GOOD" WITHIN EASY REACH.

I know when I'm feeding into rejection. I know when I am out of control, running to escape pain and fear.

Like I said, IT could be a thyroid problem, some gastric issue, or possibly even genetics, but is it possible that we're out of control with our "meds of choice" because we can't get good with us?

I know we hit this often, but we do not forfeit the love of God because we found some other way to medicate our pain. But we have to ask ourselves, *"Is this really good for me?"*

Paul said, *"I will not be mastered by anything"* (I Corinthians 6:12, NASB).

Can we honestly say that? Can we declare that food doesn't own us? What about alcohol, tobacco or sex? Those are the biggies, thus easy to spot.

How about something a little harder to recognize, like our addiction to sports, money, or our desperate need to be seen and legitimized? We might also be addicted to adventure or the need to be needed. This stuff is just as nasty as cardinal vices, yet much harder to spot.

I wonder how much of what we do for God wouldn't happen at all without the applause and admiration of man?

Are we the masters of our own appetites and desires? Do we decide what owns us? Are we aggressively seeking much healthier alternatives (inside and out)? It's worth taking a closer look.

In The Pages

What masters you? How hard is your pushback on normal negative patterns? How much internal work have you done or are you just trying to change external behavior? Is another new diet really new?

Foundations

February 24
Proverbs 24

"By wisdom a house is built, and through understanding it is established; through knowledge its rooms are filled with rare and beautiful treasures." Proverbs 24:3-4, NIV

In my first pastorate, the church experienced rapid growth. So much so, in fact, that it became evident we were going to need more space.

So we brought in a bunch of retired builders and carpenters who worked within our denomination at the state level. Most of them felt they had worked all their lives for the sole purpose of serving the local church with their craftsmanship. Like a traveling circus, they showed up on site, dragging their massive travel trailers, ready to volunteer their expertise and skill.

There were a lot of characters in that group of crusty old coots, but they could certainly throw up a building and have it ready to be painted in a week!

About a month before the team showed up, the guy who started that ministry stopped by the church to review building plans and start preparing the foundation. It was my first ever church-building project and, I have to admit, I was a little bored watching the plumbing and electrical crews dig ditches, tie steel and make the necessary preparations for the concrete pour.

After a little small talk, I blurted out, *"Dang Olin, I'm tired of messing with this foundation crap!"*[9] That little old weather-worn man looked at me with hazel blue eyes that drove stakes through to the back of my head and said,

"Boy (I was 32 years old!), *if the foundation is wrong, the building will be wrong. Then there's no reason for us to even put on our tool belts. We're building something here for the Lord; it's not an outhouse."* That pretty much ended my impatient tirade about the foundation's progress.

"Unless the Lord builds the house, they labor in vain who build it; unless the Lord guards the city, the watchman keeps awake in vain" (Psalms 127:1, NASB).

I don't know if this has ever crossed your mind or not, but the Lord is the real architect. God is the one who brings the hammers, nails and necessary materials to build His Kingdom. Even the people who get involved in a ministry or a mission opportunity are nothing more than tools in God's hands. He is the master builder.

Lady Wisdom also reminds us that she too is involved in the building process. The application of her council motivates me to be more "dialed in" to the foundation work.

As tedious as it is, we are responsible for laying down foundations with Christ as the cornerstone. Of course, this refers to character and discipline development.

One of the slogans within my spiritual community is:

"God cares more about your character than your ministry desires."

We dream big, hope big, love big, carry big passions and strong convictions about changing the world, but the foundation of character, honor, discipline and preferring others has to be right!

We aren't doing God any favors by invoking His name in our ministry quest if our character is not the solid foundation beneath what is being built! God is looking to build. Wisdom says the foundation must be right!

In The Pages

Read Psalms 89:14 and 97:2. Do you think these qualities apply to your own foundation work? How? Write out a definition of character including those qualities.

Dodging Spears

February 25
Proverbs 25

"Singing light songs to the heavyhearted is like pouring salt in their wounds." Proverbs 25:20, MSG

I suspect Solomon knew all about his father's complicated relationship with King Saul. New kings must understand the ways of old kings.

They have to be quick learners and stay wary of settling into rhythms that produce blind spots. To say it's complicated hardly does it justice. Thorny, confusing, convoluted, perplexing and bewildering, all combined, gets us somewhere in the ballpark. In looking back, what Solomon concludes is that it is dangerous to rub salt into a bleeding heart.

Saul was a tormented soul with a jutted jaw. "Unstable" pretty much summarizes the broken leader's emotional level. So the placard screams, *"Approach with caution, pay attention, a wounded spirit needs healing, not entertainment to lighten the moment."*

 Almost simultaneously with his own anointing service, David was summoned by Jonathan to minister to the weepy Saul (1 Samuel 16:14-23).

I once read that Churchill called his own bouts with depression *the black dog*. Maybe Saul was struggling with his own *black dog*, or perhaps it was deferred hope, or overwhelming regret that his replacement already stood in the wings, waiting for his departure.

Regardless of what it was, Saul was in a lot of pain. Maybe his prophetic insight sensed how it was all going to end for him? If so, the agony of Saul's less-than-glorious exit from headship was indeed enough to depress any man with an ego. It just wasn't going to end well... at all.

Just as the Spirit had undeniably anointed David, Saul felt the worst of it in *his* spirit. The weight of responsibility as king remained, but Saul knew that it was soon to be over. So David came into the presence of Israel's highest servant to minister to him with his heart and harp.

I doubt David played anything from the Hebrew pop charts. He was accustomed to playing before the Lord with an intimacy uncommon in all of Israel.

And when David was ushered in to sit with Saul, the presence of God was ushered in as well. And in that atmosphere of David welcoming the Spirit, Saul hitched a ride and got the relief he so desperately needed.

We're all familiar with the story of Job. During the first seven days, his friends were actually very helpful. They came and sat with him in all his pain and sorrow, never saying a word.

What was there to say?

The man had just lost everything. He was covered in boils. He was a pitiful specimen. It wasn't time to talk. It wasn't time to sing. It wasn't appropriate to do anything other than *just be* with that shattered man.

Every situation is different, and we need to exercise sensitivity in our response to another person's heavy heart. Often, it takes some time before people are willing to be consoled.

Don't assume that your five memorized scriptures contain a healing formula. Another frozen lasagna or your famous pound cake might not do the trick either. Don't worry if they push your plate away. Sometimes, *just you being there* is enough.

In The Pages

Do you have an automatic default while moving towards another person's pain? Who or what has really touched you when your heart has been heavy? Is food always the answer when it comes to bereavement ministry?

Pearls in Your Pocket

February 26
Proverbs 26

"Do not answer a fool according to his folly, lest you also be like him. Answer a fool according to his folly, lest he be wise in his own eyes." Proverbs 26:4-5, NKJV

"Do not give what is holy to dogs, and do not throw your pearls before swine, or they will trample them under their feet, and turn and tear you to pieces." Matthew 7:6, NASB

Patti and I have dear friends who serve as pastors to missionaries in the Middle East.[10] At one time, they were living in an apartment in downtown Cairo, but had responsibilities in more than one country.

Dave had picked up the Arabic language fairly quickly, but Sara was really struggling in hearing the guttural aspects and inflections of the dialect. Sara is a great storyteller and shared this incident in one of her email updates to her prayer partners.

Dave was out of the apartment on an errand and she could hear two men in an argument outside in the alley behind the apartment. She thought, *"What a great opportunity to listen in and glean from some of the raw emotion of the heated exchange."*

So Sara slid open the door and perched herself on the ledge just above where the dispute was happening, while carefully remaining out of sight. She really dialed into the heated conversation, picking up bits and pieces, but she soon got lost in the translation.

After about five minutes, she couldn't contain herself anymore and decided to peek over the ledge to catch a glimpse of the men causing the ruckus below. To her amazement, she discovered two small dogs fighting over food scraps in the alley!

She had indeed been listening to an argument but it wasn't exactly what she thought. It's a funny thing how strife and tension feel and sound the same, regardless of the situation.

Today's wisdom presents two contrasting thoughts: *"Do not answer a fool"* and *"Answer a fool"*. So, which is it? Actually, it's both. It's up to us to discern which is the appropriate response.

Arguing with a *"fool"*, or anyone for that matter, drags us into a life-sucking exchange that rarely settles anything. That whole *"casting your pearls"* thing is a challenge to our own personal discernment.

There are a lot of people out there who like a good debate. That's fine, as long as everyone involved is aware of the terms and benefits of the dialogue. But for any of us to try and strong-arm our beliefs onto another person who is unwilling to listen is an invitation to confrontation and a waste of our time.

What if, instead, we said, *"I have a different idea. I'd like to get your perspective on this"*? Even the presentation of the gospel or the introduction of the Holy Spirit require prudence and sensitivity.

Years of trying to help people see beyond their own religious positions has taught me that. Some of the acidity in theological jousting is just plain tiresome. Maybe it's best to keep some of your pearls in your pocket.

In The Pages

What is the biggest challenge in confronting a person who has to be right? How easy is it to stay on topic? How do you know if a person has received your correction? What about you? Can you be approached on a sensitive matter without strong pushback?

Love Wounds... (sometimes!)

February 27
Proverbs 27

"Faithful are the wounds of a friend, but deceitful are the kisses of an enemy." Proverbs 27:6, NASB

"Let the righteous strike me; it shall be a kindness. And let him rebuke me; it shall be as excellent oil; let my head not refuse it." Psalms 141:5, NKJV

One of the things I've noticed over many years of hanging around the sheep pen (church people) is that we like to quote this particular Proverb before we bring correction to a peer. When a brother or sister veers "off course," we make it our responsibility to get them back on track. So we weigh in. Heck, I did it earlier today.

Not too long ago, I commented on a Facebook declaration posted by a kid I really love. Not everyone who saw our exchange understood our relationship.

Black clouds arose quickly, full of lightning and thunder! I had challenged him on his declaration that a known leader in the body of Christ was guilty of "heresy."

After trading a couple of shots with each other publicly, we took the discussion private elsewhere. I wasn't really concerned with the theological differences. Hell, if we all have to see it the same way in order to truly love each other, we're so hosed!

My contention was that a very young Kingdom guy would call another Kingdom guy (who happens to be a gifted leader and an extremely bright thinker) a heretic. My concern was that he was wasting his energy publicly ridiculing and labeling a guy he simply didn't theologically agree with.

I'm pretty sure you can always find another person in this world who finds your personal belief system totally twisted and is more than ready to burn you at the stake for it.

Offer an opinion on any subject and see what happens! Religious devils cannot contain themselves.

You can just as easily find someone who will defend your point with you . . . to the death. The Church has more than enough issues to deal with without us airing out our theological pissiness. It's counterproductive at multiple levels.

As I said, we took the discussion offline, with cordiality and honor still in tact. I apologized for commenting publicly and he said he understood what I was trying to say. Theologically, we probably still disagree on the "why" of his opinion, but the relationship is still in tact.

But how is this possible? How can we agree to disagree and still be in fellowship?

Simple: not all wounds are fatal.

Back in the day, wandering lambs commonly had one of their legs broken by the shepherd. The shepherd would then carry the lamb and tend to all its needs.

By the time everything healed, that lamb no longer strayed from the herd or the shepherd. It was a wounding that brought a close bond.

One of the challenges God has given me with this scripture is to see it from the wounded one's vantage point. It's easy to be the one who inflicts the wound and then quotes the verse. But can we get to a place where we can graciously receive correction ourselves, honestly be grateful for another person's risk to invest in us and thank God that He loves us enough to correct us?

What if the counsel is wrong? Can we still be thankful that someone loves us enough to get *involved* in our business?

In The Pages

How well do you hear a correction? Do you speak before you see? How long does it take you to get over being offended, and appreciate the love behind the correction?

Hell Storm

February 28
Proverbs 28

"The wicked who oppress the poor are like a hailstorm that beats down the harvest." Proverbs 28:3, MSG

Some of the spring and summer thunderstorms that kick up in central Texas are absolutely awesome. They can boil up very quickly and tower over the earth for many miles.

As the warm moist air circulates at those high altitudes, it can produce hailstones the size of softballs. It's an insurance agent's nightmare and a farmer's devil.

Even the smaller storms can totally wipe out a wheat or sorghum crop in less than 10 minutes. It's not that uncommon to see automobiles in the summer looking like they've come down with a bad case of cellulite.

The worst storms produce high winds with small blocks of ice that can cave in a windshield and kill exposed livestock. Isn't it interesting how Solomon points to this ruthless weather phenomena and likens it to the heartless oppression of the poor?

Although Peterson uses the word *"wicked"*, many versions translate **rûwsh** (pronounced *roosh*) as *poor, destitute, needy and lack*. So what you have here is a poor person treating another poor person with ruthless oppression.

Instead of celebrating whatever provision they have, they look to someone less fortunate than themselves to oppress. Jesus warns us of such behavior in the parable of the unforgiving servant (Matthew 18:23-35). But just for fun, I will adjust the story to make it more relevant to today's society:

There was a waitress at the local diner who owed her employer gazillions of dollars, but was forgiven. After she was forgiven her massive and un-payable debt, the meager waitress visited her neighbor, who owed her $5.00 and a cup of sugar. The neighbor begged for mercy and leniency, but it was to no avail. The waitress had her neighbor arrested for what she owed. When news reached the waitress's employer of her pitiless refusal to forgive her neighbor's small debt, he retaliated with his own warrant for her arrest, impounded her car and demanded she pay back every penny of her debt or she would rot in jail.

It's a stretch, but here is the part we need to clue in to: the employer represents the Lord! He has paid our debts and forgiven our sins, which amounts to much more than any of us can ever repay.

When we allow ourselves to become the unforgiving waitress, oppressing others with our sour attitudes, control, lack of love and hard-heartened unforgiveness, we become as oppressive as a hailstorm on a fragile wheat crop!

In the Kingdom, we are called to be different. It has to be more than theory. It has to be real and from our heart! This kind of hellacious oppression is as cold as the ice that falls from the sky.

In The Pages

Have you ever filed legal charges on another person? Not everything is cut and dry in this world. What were your reasons for proceeding legally? When it was all over, were you satisfied with the results? Would you do the same thing again?

Love Must Speak

February 29
Proverbs 29

Happy Leap Day! I recently read that the reason for having a 29th day in February is because it takes a whole day to explain what a Leap Year is all about. The short version is that it is a slight correction to the normal calendar, so that it aligns with the astronomical calendar. So every four years, we add a day to our calendar. Traditionally, this was the designated day a woman could propose marriage to a man. Being born on Leap Day creates a few challenges, but for the most part, it's just another day to be a part of God's creation, to make a difference, to be involved in the Kingdom's progress! Today is not any more or less important than any other day. Don't waste it. Make it count! Live fully alive,

full of the Holy Spirit, sensitive to His directives, intentional with grace and love!
—MDP

"Where there is no vision, the people perish: but he that keepeth the law, happy is he." Proverbs 29:18, KJV

The Hebrew word for *"vision"* is **châzôwn** (pronounced *khaw-zone´*). It means, *"a dream, a mental image, a revelation or oracle."* It can include *sight*, but we are talking divine download here, baby!

The prophetic gifts of the Holy Spirit are a necessity, not a spiritual preference accessory, and that is exactly what Wisdom is saying here! Many would argue that the prophetic has passed away and is no longer needed now that we have the Bible. But even if that were true (and I couldn't disagree more), we would still need *"eyes to see and ears to hear"* what the Spirit has to say to us about the text.

We need help from the voice of God to illuminate, clarify and apply truth to our lives. How could we ever find our way without the voice of God? I love the words Louis Evely penned in *That Man is You*:

"Love must express and communicate itself. That is its nature. When people love one another, they start telling everything that's happened to them. Every detail of the daily life, they 'reveal' themselves to each other, unbusom themselves and exchange confidences. God hasn't ceased being Revelation any more than He's ceased being Love. He enjoys expressing Himself since He's Love. He must give Himself, share His secrets, communicate with us and reveal Himself to anyone who wants to listen."[11]

EVERYTHING IN ME SCREAMS: "YES... YES... YES!!!"

The part about *"perishing"* is not a reference to sinners dying in rebellious sin. It has everything to do with ignoring the loving voice of God and casting off the yokes of God's ways for our protection and blessing. Hearing the voice of our loving Shepherd is what leads us to the internal rest and peace we so desperately crave!

Father, give us a passion to hear your voice and heed your plans!

In The Pages

When is the last time you received a direct revelation from God? Do you pay attention to your dreams? What do you do with the illumination you get from scripture?

Heart Name

March 1
Proverbs 1

"My son, if sinners entice you, do not consent." Proverbs 1:10, NASB

In Proverbs 1:8-19, Solomon warns us of the pitfalls of peer pressure. But what I really want to talk about today is how he begins with the words, *"Hear, my son"* (V:8).

It's the first time we hear Solomon use a term of endearment. He says it again in today's text. In using the words *"my son"* he is establishing a love connection between himself and his child.

Before anything else is communicated, what God wants us to know is just how much He loves His sons and daughters. Once He's made that connection, any and all additional information can be relayed and received more effectively.

When I first began writing today's devo, I couldn't get past that first paragraph without an interruption. It is now several days later, very early in the morning.

I had a dream last night. And when I woke up, God began speaking to me about it and reminding me of the past couple weeks of my life.

Patti and I currently work with a short-term missions organization (2011), partnering with the leadership to pastor, mentor and disciple the staff. But the roles Patti and I play have more to do with going *deeper* (spiritually and emotionally) with those who pursue that from us.

The more aggressive the kids are in that pursuit, the more permission we have to cut in deep. It frees us to "call them out" into a higher purpose! And while we do "call them out," God is the only one who can actually get them to where they need to go.

Destiny is God's business... not man's.

All of this to say, the Lord showed me a few scenes from these past few weeks that revealed what happens as *we* (the learner and the teacher, the disciple and the one who disciples, the spiritual parent and spiritual son or daughter) go deeper.

I didn't realize it when it happened, but He showed me recent incidents where I have called the person I was talking to a "name of affection," rather than their birth name. To this day, my two natural daughters rarely hear me call them by their birth names.

Instead, they get some rendition of their birth name, or another name I gave them growing up, a specific name that has more "heart" in it than anything else.

I was reminded this morning of specific instances where I used someone's "heart" name a couple of times while counseling them through some moderately painful processes.

Do you ever feel like the season you are in has a theme? These past two weeks, there has been a recurring theme that keeps surfacing.

It prompts me to believe that *most* people do not know who *HE* says they are and more specifically, they don't know their own "names of affection."

> **There is nothing more life altering than hearing what your Heavenly Father says about you!**

Natural parents, spiritual parents, pastors, mentors, lovers, BFF's and even soul mates, can only implant love and truth so deep.

We need to hear the whisper of the Holy Spirit, the voice of our Father, speak our name! When we know what He calls us, we can easily receive His deeper truths about who we are and where we are going.

In The Pages

What does He call you? Don't think of the default stuff you've read in scripture. Think in terms of what you hear directly from Him. Who does He say you are? What does He say about your value to Him? Can you be still or quiet long enough to hear?

We definitely live in a time where people are much more aware and sensitive to language. Especially when it comes to references to God. Not all practicing Christians use the traditional terminology of masculine images of God. It's hard to make a case against using any other word than Son when referencing Jesus, but for God and Holy Spirit we are talking spirit here... not people. I've had to learn how to be comfortable with more inclusive language concerning the Trinity. I'm not saying you should too, but I'm suggesting that we might ought to become more aware that not everyone sees it the way that you and I might see it. It's totally okay to have your own thoughts about it, but don't assume that any notion that is contrary to yours is automatically wrong. It might not be an issue about right or wrong at all. —MDP 2018

Denying the Pass

March 2
Proverbs 2

"He guards the paths of justice, and preserves the way of His saints." Proverbs 2:8, NKJV

Please pray with me today: *Father, we thank you for your watch-care over the thousands of ministries and individuals that work with sex-trafficking and other sex-related industries. As both men and women go into those dark places all over the world to bring light, truth and hope, may firm relationships be developed in proper love and righteous respect. Keep them safe and guard their ways. May those who are counseled and befriended in such spirals of emptiness see and hear the hope that it is in YOU. Provide avenues of shrouded escape for those who want to break free. Open the doors to bring provision and supply for many who are willing to go and invest their lives in such work. Holy Spirit, cover the attempts to rescue the victims and heal the broken! Ignite our voice to NEVER-EVER be silenced!!! Show Your power, Lord! Set the captives free! In the mighty name of Jesus ! Amen!*

I was the head basketball coach for one year at a high school in East Texas. I loved the kids, but I sucked at the job.

I had played basketball in high school, but Bulldog Pride meant only one thing:

FOOTBALL!

Basketball was just something to keep you in shape until track season.

My coaches would actually "draw straws" to determine who would take on the various coaching responsibilities for basketball. It's just the way it was in a high school where football was a golden idol.

I had some experience, went to a few coaching clinics, but there is only so much you can absorb in those short sessions. You have to become a full-time student of the game and devote an enormous amount of effort to truly understand and coach basketball. As I said, I sucked at it.

I did pick up on a few things though.

One of the techniques that I implemented into my own coaching schemes was to play a defensive style that implored the strategy of "denying the pass." The defenders position themselves to simultaneously protect the basket while trying to prevent the offensive player they're guarding from getting the ball.

It's an aggressive style of defense that requires a great deal more effort than say a simple zone defense. But, it is very effective when everyone is doing his or her job!

All of that to say: God can and does "deny the pass" when aggressive saints choose to work in dark and sketchy ministry situations. He illuminates paths, prevents interference, manufactures diversion, shields and protects the way of help in righteous causes.

If you ever get the chance to talk to a missionary who needs stealthy cover from time to time, ask about God *guarding* them. I guarantee you a story or two about how HE protected or hid their way!

It's probably more common than what we think.

In The Pages

When was the last time you felt you had divine help in a ministry project? How did God show Himself in your cause? Is it far-fetched for you to believe that angels can be a source of help when we need them?

Hurts So Good

March 3
Proverbs 3

"My son, do not reject the discipline of the Lord or loathe His reproof, for whom the Lord loves He reproves, even as a father corrects the son in whom he delights." Proverbs 3:11-12, NASB

So, this is the sixth time we've heard Solomon say, *"my son"* since he started the writings. He continues to drill home the fact that the *relationship* is important to him. *Then* he brings the teaching, the correction, the truth, out of the shadows.

I was thinking in the shower today about how we preface correction or discipline with the people we love. I remember when I was still a viable and deserving candidate for youthful discipline, I would be sent to my room for an agonizing amount of time, which was then followed up with "the talk" and/or punishment.
  It always began with, *"Son, you know I love you* (truth). *This is going to hurt me*

more than it hurts you (felt like bullshit to me), *but..."*

That "but" would be the lead-in to questions about why I did what I did, me saying nothing too helpful in pleading my case, a reminder of what was promised if I disobeyed and then the actual punishment I knew beforehand I would get if I acted out, and usually acted out anyway.

I have done the exact same thing to my kids (both spiritual and natural). Not the punishment stuff, but the tough talks. My assumption here deduces that we all probably do a better-than-average job of confirming our love when we are disciplining or *weighing in* to tense situations with someone important to us.

But, how often do we just say, *"I love you"* for no reason at all? Do we actually tell our friends, *"You are very important to me"* or *"I see you, I hear you, I care"*?

I'm not even sure why this surfaced today, but maybe I (maybe *we*) need to be reminded that we don't need a reason or a strategy for communicating our true feelings towards the people we love.

Granted, there is nothing like a little lovin' before you drop the hammer to ease the blow, but people need their lives interrupted with God's love, through you, on a regular basis! We don't have to have a reason to say the words—let's just speak and confirm.

There are so many lessons about the loving reproof of the Lord we can apply using scripture. Correction and the discipline are for whom He delights!

He is not an angry God, out of control in his correction. It is training, protection and real help in our development. He's not being mean.

Currently (2011) I have two grandchildren. They are almost three years old. They will walk alongside you and hold your hand, but if they see something they like, or want, or get too excited to contain themselves, they will break away and run straight towards that thing that has their attention.

If it's a puppy across the street, they do not check for traffic, they do not look both ways; they just run. They have to be taught, sternly at times, that it is not in their best interest to behave in that manner.

We big people have to be taught too. We are all sons and daughters. He loves us, and He shows us His love in many different ways. Our job is to receive that love as best as we can, keeping it at the forefront of our hearts. Our Father loves us. He tells us and shows us constantly.

In The Pages

Are you a person who can understand love in the midst of pain? How were you disciplined as a child? Is it possible it affects your God image? How?

18 Holes of Hell

March 4
Proverbs 4

"Take firm hold of instruction, do not let go; keep her, for she is your life." Proverbs 4:13, NKJV

"Grip it and rip it!" I hadn't heard that one before.

A kid, a frikk'n kid, a gifted athlete (who once threw for 646 yards in a single game, as quarterback for a respected Division I football team), was taunting me like the baggy-jeaned old coot I felt like during that round of golf.[12]

With the wind behind me, in the clean, thin mountain air, I was about to hit my best shot of the day, off an elevated tee box, no less. He had out-driven me almost 20 yards on a consistent basis all day. I was getting tired of the heckling.

As I approached my ball, I heard him say, *"Grip it and rip it!"* I interpreted this as, *"Don't have a heart attack gramps. Go ahead, risk fudging your Huggie and swing hard!"* So I told myself, *"Normal swing... head down... good contact... don't try to kill it,"* and obliged him with a smoking drive right down the middle of the fairway.

I've been playing this game for most of my life and I can tell you with confidence, my ball was easily 300+ yards out there. Daddy was feeling good! So when Cody teed it up next, I said, *"Rip it yourself."* So he did.

As we drove up in our carts to find his ball about 35 yards in front of mine, Cody asked me, *"Hey Mike, have you heard about the new Walmart that's going to be built in this neighborhood?"* I should have seen it coming. *"No. What about it?"* With his charming grin and devil-like shark eyes glaring, *"They're going to build it on the parcel of land between your ball and mine."*

Of course our cart partners were laughing their butts off by now, so I grunted, *"Just what this world needs, another smart-ass kid."* Sheesh! You would have thought he'd just won the Masters or something. Long day. Where was that frikk'n beer cart?

"Grip it and rip it" works. Wisdom is the subject. Solomon is talking to his kids about holding tight to the truth, building their lives around those precious helps, and guarding those delicacies of God as if their lives depended on it.

Once, on a trip to Africa, I had my eldest daughter, Nicole, with me. She was young, beautiful and quite the novelty. I would get slightly nervous if she ventured too far from my sight.

When we would get into ministry situations where hundreds of people would line up for prayer, I would make arrangements with the pastor for someone to keep an eye on Nicole. I couldn't be in two places at once.

I didn't think too much about my defensive posture while we were in Africa. I was just doing what dads do.

A couple of months later, that same African pastor came to visit us at the church I had started in Texas. He couldn't help but laugh as he told my congregation how I had protected Nicole in Africa like she was an egg.

At first, I thought that was a silly analogy. But then I remembered that most of my "compensation" in those villages had been chickens, corn, but mostly eggs. What they gave was indeed fragile, but precious to them.

My daughter was precious to me, so I'll admit I could have been a bit paranoid and grossly over protective, but we usually take care with what is precious to us, right?

Solomon wanted his sons and daughters to clutch tightly to wisdom. He knew the course before them came with challenges, traps and peril. Wisdom is long and straight, right down the middle. Keep your head down and ignore the chatter. Focus. Grip it and rip it!

In The Pages

How intent are you in the pursuit of wisdom? Who is speaking into your life, your struggles or your plans? Who are you speaking into? A person seeking your counsel can draw stuff from the deep wells in you that you forgot were down in there. Share what you got and then ask the Lord for more!

Groaning

March 5
Proverbs 5

"She does not ponder the path of life; her ways are unstable, she does not know it." Proverbs 5:6, NASB

"And you groan at your final end, when your flesh and your body are consumed; and you say, 'How I have hated instruction! And my heart spurned reproof! I have not listened to the voice of my teachers, nor inclined my ear to my instructors! I was almost in utter ruin in the midst of the assembly and congregation." Proverbs 5:11-14, NASB

I recently read a disturbing article:

Every year, 19 million people are infected with a sexually transmitted disease. Among them, half are young adults between the ages of 15 and 24, according to the Centers for Disease Control and Prevention (CDC). However, many cases of STDs go undiagnosed, so it's possible that the numbers are much higher. Meanwhile, it's estimated that STDs like chlamydia, gonorrhea, and syphilis cost the United States nearly $15 billion every year in direct medical costs, the CDC states. (STD Facts and Figures: Which are Most Common and Other Essential Statistics, (2008), from sixwise.com)

Today's verses are about the destructive patterns associated with adultery, but the entire chapter is super-charged with instructions from Wisdom on how to avoid lustful liaisons outside of marital covenant. Yes, yes, it's very old fashioned and possibly even unrealistic by modern sentiment, but there are more reasons to heed Wisdom's advice on this other than, *"Because the Bible says so, doofus!"*

I don't need to beat the purity drum here. We all know it's bad out there.

My daughter is a Nurse Practitioner in a Women's Clinic. The people and things she sees on a regular basis only confirm the warning of the *groaning* that happens when sexual disease "afflicts" a person's life.

The ministry Patti and I do for the Lord allows us a lot of face time with young men and women who are on fire for the Kingdom of God. But, too many of them are dealing with these horrendous physical issues due to mistakes they made in either their impatience or impulse.

I'm talking about cream-of-the-crop kids! They are bright, intelligent, full of hope, desiring a mate, hungry for God-given covenant and ready to receive the man or woman of their dreams. But, at the same time, they are dreading the inevitable moment of having to disclose their experiences with herpes, genital warts, Hepatitis, or whatever else plagues them.

That feeling of unwanted shame—of being broken, dirty and unclean—never strays too far from their head or heart.

As a pastor and a father, I feel the need to repent to young men and women. We may have told you to abstain, but we didn't have the courage to tell you why. *"Because the Bible says..."* just isn't enough of a reason in our culture.

In fact, if that's the only message you've got to give... then your message blows.

You deserved the real truth about soul ties, sexual hygiene, generational sin and every other topic we weren't sure you could handle. We fulfilled the bare minimum of our obligation.

Maybe we didn't have our own lust issues under control and didn't know what to say. Whatever the case, please forgive us. Forgive me! Let's start the healing there. Lust and all the ugly effects that go along with it don't have to have the final say.

In The Pages

So, are you afflicted with anything? If so, how much spiritual work have you done with your issue? Is it all still a secret? Nothing gets the caress of hell like a secret.

Pray for strength to get some help—some real, honest, loving, spiritual help. Confession turns on the Light to disarm the condemning lies of darkness. HE is healer and author of our wholeness!

If not, whom do you know that is struggling with these issues? What have you done to encourage them to seek help? They need an understanding friend.

It Flows Down

March 6
Proverbs 6

"Who with perversity in his heart continually devises evil, who spreads strife. Therefore his calamity will come suddenly; instantly he will be broken and there will be no healing." Proverbs 6:14-15, NASB

"Riffraff and rascals talk out of both sides of their mouths. They wink at each other, they shuffle their feet, they cross their fingers behind their backs. Their perverse minds are always cooking up something nasty, always stirring up trouble. Catastrophe is just around the corner for them, a total smashup, their lives ruined beyond repair." Proverbs 6:12-15, MSG

Part of my exegetical training taught me that the word *"therefore"* prompts the question, "what is the *therefore,* there for?" It's a little play on words to stimulate a deeper digging into what prefaced the summary thought.

Solomon makes a pretty bleak prophetic declaration in verse 15. In verses 12-14, he describes the "DNA," or character traits of the worthless, or *evil* person. What jump-started my direction today is the latter part of verse 14 in the (NASB): *"...continually devises evil, who spreads strife. THEREFORE..."* The domino effect eventually culminates in verse 15. Yeah, it's ugly.

I mentioned earlier the prophetic nature of verse 15. 2 Chronicles 9 ends with the final details of Solomon's reign as King of Israel and his death. The rest of the book is about the Davidic dynasty, the kingdom of Israel's tragic split into two separate tribes and 70 years of Babylonian captivity.

Beginning with Rehoboam taking the throne (which is where the strife and division began), each king is mentioned by name, age, the number of years he ruled and a commentary on whether or not he honored the Lord. There isn't much confusion about how the theocracy judged its leadership:

"So King Rehoboam strengthened himself in Jerusalem and reigned. Now Rehoboam was forty-one years old when he began to reign, and he reigned seventeen years in Jerusalem, the city which the Lord had chosen from all the tribes of Israel, to put His name there. And his mother's name was Naamah the Ammonitess. **He did evil because he did not set his heart to seek the Lord**" (2 Chronicles 12:13-14, NASB).

Nice, huh?

Good, solid, civil engineering theory tells us that sewage flows downhill. *Calamity* comes down *suddenly* because of whatever happened up there. Stuff breaks over here, because of what happened over there. *Strife* spreads among the common because of the disunity of the select. It's like a bad stomach virus. Vomitville for everyone!

But here is my own personal challenge (feel free to challenge yourself with it as well):

I HAVE TO TAKE RESPONSIBILITY FOR ME

Which means I can't blame and point to what is over me, above me, or prior to me and just settle for less than what I know I am responsible for now.

We need to take dominion over whatever it is that we lead. What happened before us is beyond our control. But for what follows us, we can have an impact on that outcome now.

I do not have to stir up strife. I do not have to be in disunity. I can choose to honor the Lord with true love and respect for others!

In The Pages

If you knew your history in leadership was going to be in print for all to see, for all time, would you do it differently? Do a little inventory in 2 Chronicles (specifically chapters 10 through 36) and decide for yourself what distinguished the good from the bad. It's worth a look!

Divine Chaperone

March 7
Proverbs 7

"Say to wisdom, 'You are my sister,' and call understanding your nearest kin, that they may keep you from the immoral woman, from the seductress who flatters with her words." Proverbs 7:4-5, NKJV

There is nothing like trying to make out with your prom date with your little sister or brother sitting in the back seat to offer their commentary. I had a little sister *and* a little brother. Both of them were horrible for my romantic aspirations, but perfect for some preventive accountability.

Between the nonstop chatter of two, half-naked Barbie dolls and the make-believe roaring of super-charged Hot Wheels, I can see how those kinds of distractions could have been beneficial to me back in the day before I knew anything about real love.

That is what Solomon is saying here. Allow Lady Wisdom to be your sister, your intimate confidante, who keeps you safe when things are a little too hot to handle. I know it feels like overkill, but the temptations of immorality and seduction are real!

Solomon wants someone who loves us to watch over us. If it isn't another person, then Lady Wisdom herself will hold us accountable. We need that kind of help sometimes.

I like the fact that Solomon suggests we get some additional help. The reason this makes so much sense is because immorality, temptation and seduction all want to see us fall.

"Be of sober spirit, be on the alert. Your adversary, the devil, prowls around like a roaring lion, seeking someone to devour" (1 Peter 5:8, NASB).

Our enemy searches for ways to circumvent our progress, our development, our peace and our foundations for rest, hope and love. He hates us. BUT our Father loves us. So we are challenged to be proactive in protecting ourselves and live honorably in our relationships.

Lust always demands immediate satisfaction
(*It's not always sexual. Lust can be for power, control, recognition and riches.*)

Lust does not care who or what it destroys.

Its only plan is to have what it wants.

"So she seizes him and kisses him and with a brazen face she says to him: I was due to offer peace offerings; today I have paid my vows. Therefore I have come out to meet you, to seek your presence earnestly, and I have found you. I have spread my couch with coverings, with colored linens of Egypt. I have sprinkled my bed with myrrh, aloes and cinnamon. Come, let us drink our fill of love until morning; let us delight ourselves with caresses" (Proverbs 7:13-18, NASB).

See? The plan is to get what she wants, no matter the cost.

One more thought here: Often, it is common for the word *sister* to be used as a synonym for *wife* (Song of Solomon 4:9-10, 12; 5:1-2).

For you married couples: are you filling your mind and spirit with the sweet memories of your many intimacies with your mate?

A good dose of rich memory leaves little room for the vain imaginations and lustful illusions of immoral schemes.

A memory can kick a fantasy's butt every frikk'n time! Let your love leave a lasting impression! It can be a time-honored chaperone in the dry times of life!

In The Pages

Sir, when you are dating and courting that Godly woman, are you taking responsibility for setting and honoring the boundaries for her healthy self-respect and purity?

Sweet lady, will you follow that kind of strong lead and capitalize on your protection, or do you need to seduce in order to keep your security?

Married? When was the last time (if ever) you studied the Song of Solomon? It's a great study!

I Was Before I Was

March 8
Proverbs 8

"I have been established from everlasting, from the beginning, before there was ever an earth." Proverbs 8:23, NKJV

"Now, Father, glorify Me together with Yourself, with the glory which I had with You before the world was." John 17:5, NASB

This isn't the first time we've touched on this, and it probably won't be the last. Go back and re-read the words of Jesus very slowly.

Now, read today's proverb again. Do you see a parallel?

Before the world was *"established",* or **nâçak** (pronounced naw-sak´), which means, *"created, poured out, formed, or set up"*, Wisdom existed. The only other place in scripture where this Hebrew word is used is in Psalms 2:6: *"But as for Me, I have installed My King upon Zion, My holy mountain"* (NASB).

It's the exact same Hebrew word and here it also implies *"consecration, ordination, anointing or appointment."*

Proverbs 8:24-31 confirms that there was a whole lot going on before the earth was actually formed. Solomon says that Wisdom was right in the midst of the entire creation process. He also says that Wisdom was set up and operational from *everlasting.*

The Hebrew word for *"everlasting"* is **ôlâm** (pronounced *o-lawm´*) meaning, *"before time as we know it, time outside of our minds, perpetually before and perpetually behind,"* or what we call *"eternity."* Maybe someone very bright could explain all this with complicated math formulas, but the point is that somewhere in all of that pre-creation *glory* Jesus speaks of, we find divine communication of the Godhead, manifested in the mind of Christ, and vocalized by the Holy Spirit.

Paul confirms it,

"In the same way the Spirit also helps our weakness; for we do not know how to pray as we should, but the Spirit Himself intercedes for us with groanings too deep for words; and He who searches the hearts knows what the mind of the Spirit is, because He intercedes for the saints according to the will of God" (Romans 8:26-27, NASB).

Limited space allows me to push no further today, but just know that this same divine voice and mind of Wisdom is available to you and me today. When we ask for wisdom, we should expect the voice of the Holy Spirit to confirm that wisdom is already in our heart and mind. It is a beautiful thing, really!

God said to Jeremiah, *"Before I formed you in the womb I knew you, and before you were born I consecrated you; I have appointed you a prophet to the nations"* (Jeremiah 1:5, NASB). God intimately knew, consecrated, ordained and anointed Jeremiah to be a prophet before he was even inside his mother's body!

I'm not grinding a political ax here, but I'm trying to get our hearts and minds around THAT truth! If wisdom was in place before anything else was formed, it doesn't seem to me to be a stretch that we were all in His heart before we took habitat inside of our mother's womb.

From the depths of eternity, Wisdom prepared itself to be available to us. We ask, the Spirit speaks and we become the manifest mind of Christ.

In The Pages

Have you ever talked with a person who was almost killed, aborted, or lived through some life-threatening experience? What is his or her understanding about the Divine purpose of each and every person? What is your own understanding about God's creative purpose for your life?

Brilliantly Stupid

March 9
Proverbs 9

"Stolen water is refreshing; food eaten in secret tastes the best! But little do they know that the dead are there. Her guests are in the depths of the grave." Proverbs 9:17-18, NIV

I love the Darwin Awards. Every year, some ambiguous yet authoritative person compiles the best of the worst stories about stupid things people do to themselves. Most of the stories are so ridiculous it's hard to believe they really happened.

My personal favorite is the story of two guys who were out coon hunting after dark. Their old pickup truck blew a fuse and lost its use of the headlights. Of course there were no spare fuses available, and since they were desperate for a quick fix, they decided with brilliant ingenuity and southern improvising that a shell from the .22 caliber rifle would be the perfect substitution.

Conventional wisdom declares, *"It's all good until somebody gets hurt!"* Evidently, using a .22 cartridge wasn't such a good idea after all. It seems that shell got really hot as an electrical conductor and fired off from inside the fuse box!

The lead tip pinged around inside the cab of the truck several times before it managed to find "home, sweet home" inside of the driver's left testicle! Since steering was now no longer a priority, the truck and it's rattled passengers crashed through a fence and landed in a local farmer's grain bin.

Can you imagine the EMT guys trying to keep a straight face once they got the scoop? I'm from the south, so I have no doubt in my mind of this story's truth.

"Dale, get me another beer would ya? Damn, this thing is bleedin'! Well... we better call someone and tell 'em I shot myself in the huevos."

Jesus help us. God's children are strange creatures!

Today's text is about potential candidates for the Darwin Awards, in the category of "Sexual Sins." Solomon is talking about the devastation of sexual conduct outside of marriage.

On the front end, the *"stolen water"* (sexual intercourse with someone who is not your mate) is *"refreshing" (maybe even downright exhilarating),* and the *"food eaten in secret"* (the substance of the little infraction) tastes good to the palate.

But, "it's all good, until somebody gets hurt!" If you search scripture, you'll often find the word "pleasure" attached to the word "sin" (2 Tim 3:4; Titus 3:3; Hebrews 11:25). God isn't a killjoy or a prude.

Please try to remember that He inserted multiple "pleasure triggers" into our sexual functionality! But there is a proper context in order to enjoy the full benefits of those triggers physically, emotionally and spiritually.

The pleasure of physical sexual contact was His specific design, which is why it's such a priority for mankind! It's part of what holds marriage and covenant together!

Bluntly, it is just STUPID to operate sexually outside of the boundaries of marriage, especially with all we know!

"The devil will make you stupid." Ever heard that? Forrest Gump's mama said, *"Stupid is as stupid does."* Eventually, we're going to have to pay the price for our less-than-brilliant affairs and irresponsible decisions.

I had a dear friend who slid out one night for a little hanky-panky and left the hotel receipt in the glove box of his car. His wife found the receipt while reaching for a Kleenex the very next day! Can you say, BUSTED?

The *"depths of the grave"* and the pain involved with these kinds of risks are just NOT WORTH IT!

In The Pages

What is the stupidest thing you've ever done? Was it worth it? What were the consequences? What did you learn from your mistake? Has it changed your life?

Deceit, Hate, & Lies

March 10
Proverbs 10

"Whoever hides hate is a liar. Whoever tells lies is a fool." Proverbs 10:18, NCV

"He who hates, disguises it with his lips, and lays up deceit within himself; when he speaks kindly, do not believe him, for there are seven abominations in his heart; though his hatred is covered by deceit, his wickedness will be revealed before the assembly." Proverbs 26:24-26, NKJV

A *"liar"* is not to be trusted. That's obvious. But it rarely dawns on us that *"hate"* is the root of deception.

We're not talking about the cover-up of a child to keep from getting in trouble for stealing gum at the grocery store. What Solomon is referencing here is calculated deception.

It may manifest as a smile or a pat on the back, but it intends to bring you harm. Hate is the source of that kind of poison.

Most of the people I've ever known who could tell a lie as easily as they tell the truth are people who have a very hateful side of themselves. They don't like to be crossed. They've been wounded, rejected or wronged by someone close to them.

Bitterness has lingered for so long without resolution that demonic hate has taken over and become a stronghold in their life. They are capable of smiling at you while yanking out your heart, without regret. God still loves them, but this is about as ugly as mankind ever gets.

In all of about 15 minutes, HE had pretty much blown up every spiritual and social paradigm they had ever known. He put a chainsaw to their sacred cows, the ones they had housed and fed their entire lives! How were they to understand this man and how he talked?

Jesus said, *"You have heard that it was said, 'You shall love your neighbor and hate your enemy'"* (Matthew 5:43, NASB).

He was right! They had heard this taught via the *lex talionis,* or the "Law of Retaliation" (Exodus 21:24; Leviticus 24:20; Deuteronomy 19:21).

The Law commanded that you love your neighbor (Leviticus 19:18), but retaliate with equal force against anyone who messes with you. That was their way.

But Jesus dropped a bombshell: *"But I say to you, love your enemies and pray for those who persecute you, so that you may be sons of your Father who is in heaven"* (Matthew 5:44-45, NASB). They must have been thinking, *"What in the Sam hell did he just say? Did you hear that? What kind of man is this?"* Then He explains why:

"If all you do is love the lovable, do you expect a bonus? Anybody can do that. If

you simply say hello to those who greet you, do you expect a medal? Any run-of-the-mill sinner does that. In a word, what I'm saying is, grow up. You're kingdom subjects. Now live like it. Live out your God-created identity. Live generously and graciously toward others, the way God lives toward you" (Matthew 5:46-48, MSG).

The deception must stop; the hater must forgive and our love needs to be real!

In The Pages

Do you know people who can't always seem to tell the truth? The nature of a liar is described in John 8:44. What new revelation did you gain from today's devo? How does it apply to your life?

Scatter

March 11
Proverbs 11

"One man gives freely, yet gains even more; another withholds unduly, but comes to poverty. A generous man will prosper; he who refreshes others will himself be refreshed." Proverbs 11:24-25, NASB

"The world of the generous gets larger and larger; the world of the stingy gets smaller and smaller. The one who blesses others is abundantly blessed; those who help others are helped." Proverbs 11:24-25, MSG

We rarely choose faith. We need to be reminded of this on a regular basis. God calls us into faith. And if we agree to go on this journey, and to trust Him (we all have our good days and bad days), we realize that we end up in *His* faith on the matter.

I vaguely remember how God orchestrated an unexplainable series of events that led me, at the right time, in the right way, through a maze of twists and turns, which prepared my heart and my head to really see Him. The maze He led me through is what prompted me to receive the gift of forgiveness through Christ.

He gave me the eyes to see. He gave me the courage to believe. He gave me instant verification and the undeniable affirmation that my sins had all been forgiven. Just like that, I was different. And I knew it was all because of Him. I was absolutely unaware of my own faith. I was only aware of what He was calling me to believe.

From the very moment of that tiny seed transaction of His faith and His grace, exploding inside of my grungy heart, in a very small campus apartment in Fayetteville, Arkansas, on May 28, 1978, my walk and communion with God has only increased each and every day. God's generosity has continually expanded over my life. I simply believe the truth of today's Proverb.

The NASB says, *"There is one who scatters, yet increases all the more"*. The Hebrew word for *"scatters"* is **pâzar** (pronounced *paw-zar'*), and it means, *"to disperse abroad in charitable causes, not investments or agro-centric purpose."*

The *NET Bible Commentary* offers this remarkable truth,

> *"This is a paradox:* **Generosity determines prosperity in God's economy.***"*

My friend Pastor David Johnson says it this way:

"When you sow resources into the Kingdom, you reap a Kingdom reward. The items given or received back are relevant to their needs and our needs. God makes those determinations of how the blessing and increase arrives." [13]

I can live with that!

I also love the fact that there are people who get this truth, but have absolutely no spiritual understanding of these dynamics. They are just generous—they love to give—and they understand how fortunate they are with what they have been able to compile. There is certain "freshness" about a person's life who lives as a giver. We are easily drawn to them and evidently, so are abundant blessings!

Notice, Solomon doesn't restrict the principle to just "Kingdom" or "God" people. Surely, we (His created sons and daughters) all have eyes to see the wisdom in living this way! Surely, we want God's generosity continually expanding over our lives each and every day!

In The Pages

Would the people around you characterize you as generous? What kind of Kingdom rewards have you seen returned to you because of your giving? In the Hebrew, *generous man* means "the soul of blessing." Is that you?

Dump It

March 12
Proverbs 12

I'm a hot mess right now. Row 21, seat F, 31,000 feet up in the air, and a total wreck! As Patti and I were waiting in line to board our plane, a Ft. Carson soldier was kissing his wife and two sons (maybe ages 10 and 13) goodbye for his third tour in Iraq. We've seen the homemade "welcome home" signs lots of times. Those moments are always fun to watch, exciting and emotional. But this was almost unbearable. The other soldiers standing around barely noticed. They've seen it too many times. I looked at Patti and could see the tears gathering. I too was swallowing large bites of undigested raw emotion. It was hard to watch.

The sacrifice of men and women who wear Uncle Sam's uniform is not to be taken lightly. I haven't always noticed, and I'm ashamed to admit that. I remember crying for days after I saw "Saving Private Ryan." I was totally in the dark about war in general, so I started reading all about what it really costs (in blood, lives and tears) to defend our nation. Before we crack open our mind and heart to another devo today, let's just stop and take a moment to thank God for the men and women who have answered "the call" to serve this country in our nation's uniform.

Please pray for them, pray for their families, pray for their parents, pray for our veterans, and pray for our nation's leaders who bear the burden of putting our loved ones, our favorite sons and daughters, our finest, in harm's way! Pray for those who are recovering (or who never will recover) from their wounds and various scars of duty! We owe them the best of what we have to offer! We owe them our heartfelt thanks! -MDP-

"Anxiety in the heart of man causes depression, but a good word makes it glad." Proverbs 12:25, NKJV

There isn't a whole lot to say here. It is what it is. Plain as day, right there it sits, like an inflamed zit:

Anxiety in the heart of man causes depression.

The Hebrew word for *"anxiety"* is **d^e'âgâh** (pronounced *děh-aw-gaw´*) meaning, *"a heaviness or sorrow that is rooted in fear."* Depression can also manifest because of deep-seated anger. But here, it's more out of fear.

Fear of what, you ask? Primarily, we're afraid that God either doesn't see our problem or He isn't concerned enough to do anything about our problem. So it becomes all about us taking control. And if it is too big for us to manage, our fear becomes anxiety. Anxiety fixes nothing.

I'm fairly convinced that the bulk of physical afflictions we suffer as a society are due to the amount of stress, anxiety and fear we carry in our spirits!

We simply will not trust God to take care of us.

Solutions? Here's a couple:

"Therefore humble yourselves under the mighty hand of God, that He may exalt you at the proper time, casting all your anxiety on Him, because He cares for you" (1 Peter 5:6-7, NASB).

"Be anxious for nothing, but in everything by prayer and supplication with thanksgiving let your requests be made known to God. And the peace of God, which surpasses all comprehension, will guard your hearts and your minds in Christ Jesus" (Philippians 4:6-7, NASB).

In The Pages

What is pushing your anxiety/fear button today? Maybe it's time to dump some of this concern into the lap of Jesus. He does know and see your concern!

Favor, Lord!

March 13
Proverbs 13

"Good understanding produces favor, but the way of the treacherous is hard. Every prudent man acts with knowledge, but a fool displays folly." Proverbs 13:15-16, NASB

I like the whole *"produces favor"* thought. A little divine help would do us all some good. We smile at that notion, but it really is how we feel.

Most of us call out for "favor" because we want preferential treatment from God. We want Him to show us the shortcuts, the easier paths, the hidden trails that bring ease and comfort. Trust me, when I'm waiting on an upgrade from the airline on an overseas trip, I'm screaming for FAVOR because I want the comfort! That's cool, but when we really start claiming that favor, we might want to consider the possibility that it's **tied to His purpose**.

We got that *favor* for a reason. We get His *favor* because it helps us accomplish *His* mission much more efficiently and effectively!

God really does like us and He does bless us, but He does that for everyone! We are all His children. But He doesn't dish out *favor* because we're in His "preferred" status club.

He gives *favor* because He's anointing our ways to accomplish His purpose!

Acting with knowledge, operating by prudence, committing to living under His influence, all produce favor for us because these things are in alignment with God's highest desire for our lives. People who situate their passions and goals with Kingdom agenda get help from the influence of the King. It makes simple and logical sense to expect favor when we are doing His agenda.

"The fear of the Lord is the beginning of wisdom; a good understanding have all those who do His commandments; His praise endures forever" (Psalms 111:10, NASB).

People with *"good understanding"* are reflective people who have worked hard for the insights they have. They have good sense, they make good judgments and they live in the discipline of self-governance.

People like this are motivated by purpose and driven by goals to capitalize on what they recognize God has already blessed them with. They steward their lives and make the most of their opportunities!

Wisdom says this *way*, this general attitude, this methodology generates His favor! He ordains and discharges His favor to accompany these kinds of people because they're headed in a direction aligned with His overall purpose.

*"Day by day continuing with one mind in the temple, and breaking bread from house to house, they were taking their meals together with gladness and sincerity of heart, praising God and **having favor** with all the people. And the Lord was adding to their number day by day those who were being saved"* (Acts 2:46-47, NASB).

I want you to see that their overall way, their rightful stewardship of what God had given them, was in alignment with God's overall purpose to bring people to Kingdom. That's the "why" of *favor*. His purpose!

Our living with and acting upon that *"good understanding"* will produce more favor for you and me.

In The Pages

Do you have your own definition of favor? Where do you need His favor right now in your life? Are you in cooperation with His way for that favor? What kind of changes do you need to make to get into alignment with Him?

Camping Blessed

March 14
Proverbs 14

"The house of the wicked will be destroyed, but the tent of the upright will flourish." Proverbs 14:11, NASB

"The house of the wicked is destroyed, and the tent of the upright flourisheth." Proverbs 14:11, YLT

Today's verse is part of a 4-verse package (verses 11-14) addressing the notion that appearance can be deceiving. This is especially true when the "strong and mighty" become reckless and devoid of respect for responsibility and its influence on the "trickle-down" of authority.

This week, the national headlines have been full of buzz because a very prominent guy got reckless and stupid in his personal life. It cost him his job ($3.5 million a year in salary and benefits) and possibly his family. Because of the nature of his position, thousands of people have been affected and disappointed.

Young and old have muttered, "WTH?" What appeared to be a small empire of success has been torched in an instant. People will recover. "One monkey doesn't stop the show." But, WOW! For this guy, life will never be the same.

Let's be clear about this. It wasn't over when the guy got fired. The "beginning of the end" started when little covert decisions were being made months, maybe even years earlier.

Young's translation boldly declares that the *"house of the wicked"* is already destroyed. Sure, it might be standing tall today, spouting its strength, building its towers high, but don't be fooled by what you see with your eyes—it's already rubble.

Conversely, just because something doesn't appear very strong, mighty, popular, or on the "trendy edge," doesn't mean it's weak or ineffective. Paul said, *"For we walk by faith, not by sight"* (2 Corinthians 5:7, NASB). We live out of our relational experiences with the Lord, not because we're influenced by the world's paradigms.

"Uprightness" doesn't have to appear gloriously pious. Often times, it seems to finish in the middle of the pack. Obviously, a tent can be easily knocked down by harsh elements. But again, Wisdom's declaration projects end results that are full of God's blessings because of our choices to live uprightly.

Resilience is one of the prime benefits of a tent. To *"flourish"* means *"to grow, spread, bud out and blossom in abundance."*

Because Lady Wisdom's default foundation is *"The fear of the Lord is the beginning of wisdom"* (Proverbs 9:10, NASB), we are led to believe that God will build our house *with* us, according to our desires to honor the ultimate design. Whether a cathedral, castle, tent, shack or shanty, if it is full of His goodness and blessing, what more could we possibly ask for?

In The Pages

Check out these verses: Isaiah 14:22-23; Job 14:9; and Psalms 92:12-15. Compiling all the data, what impressions do you get about the intentionality of the Lord towards blessing the house of the upright?

Bulldozing Pride

March 15
Proverbs 15

"The Lord tears down the proud man's house but he keeps the widow's boundaries intact." Proverbs 15:25, NIV

The few, the proud, the Marines! It's a great advertisement for that particular branch of our armed forces.

The intense brotherhood of these macho, chisel-chinned warriors sends the message that they are elite, specialized and prepared for just about any job they have to do. Talk to any Marine vet and he'll confirm your preconceived notions about all that.

When we consider the "why" of their existence, we see that *pride* is a part of their preparation and commitment to the details of either keeping the peace, or waging war. The world knows American Marines are trained to fight in every condition known to man and that is what makes them so feared (and an emblem of our country's power).

We kind of want them to be like that, don't we?

My high school football coaches made "pride" their motto for growing us up as young men. It usually required going against the current of trendy culture: short haircuts when all the "cool" guys had long hair, keeping our shirt tails tucked in (lame), shoes polished on game days and keeping the locker room clean. Even the smallest infractions earned us massive disciplinary action. It was how the coaches kept order in the ranks; a very necessary element in the examples I've provided.

But while taking pride in details is one thing, **the pride of life** or **the pride of man** is a whole different matter! Today's text weighs in heavily on the perils of a *prideful* person.

The kind of pride today's text is referring to is **gê'eh** (pronounced *gay-eh'*), which means *"pure arrogance."* The Lord is very active in coming against the *pride* of *man*. He *tears down* what the arrogance of man builds up:

"They said to one another, 'Come, let us make bricks and burn them thoroughly.' And they used brick for stone, and they used tar for mortar. Then they said, 'Come, let us build for ourselves a city, and a tower whose top will reach into heaven, and let us make for ourselves a name, otherwise we will be scattered abroad over the face of the whole earth'" (Genesis 11:3-4, NASB).

I honestly do not think the tower was the issue. God knew they couldn't reach Him with what they could build with their own hands. He wasn't threatened by their using their God-given abilities was He?

The problem was that little phrase, *"Let us make for ourselves a name."* They wanted to establish their own fame! They too wanted to be worshiped by man. God understood this as arrogant rebellion by the Shinarites.

IT WAS THEIR PUSH-AWAY FROM HIS TABLE.

He responds in effect, *"If I let them get away with this kind of arrogant pride, where will it stop?"* (Genesis 11:6).

Ambitious pride usually doesn't stop until God intervenes!

I had a young man recently tell me he wanted to *"lead a movement."* When I asked him why, he was silent. Evidently no one had ever challenged him about that thought. Thirty seconds later he finally replied, *"That probably has more to do with my reputation than God's, huh?"*

That's a pretty big revelation for a young guy. Hope it sticks.

In The Pages

How much of what man has physically built (especially in the Name of God) do you think was actually mandated by God? Does God require the ornate habitation and comfort for worship and prayer to count? Then why do we do it?

This is one of those places where I may have some different thoughts on this subject now. I do believe that God can and does intervene in our lives. Many times it happens without our knowledge. BUT, I'm not convinced that every negative and positive outcome is divinely orchestrated. The natural/normal byproduct of pride can be ruthlessly scathing. The natural/normal byproduct of love can be gloriously beautiful. Sometimes it's not God at work. Sometimes it's us. —MDP 2018

Dicey Dice

March 16
Proverbs 16

"The lot is cast into the lap, but its every decision is from the Lord." Proverbs 16:33, NASB

The *Commentary Critical and Explanatory on the Whole Bible* offers the following about today's text: "Seemingly the most fortuitous events are ordered by God." That was the overall impression when it came to *casting lots*, a roll of the dice whose outcome was determined by God.

We can read all throughout scripture where lots were used to determine some end result (Numbers 26:5; Jonah 1:7; Ezekiel 48:29; John 19:24; Acts 1:26). To me, the stretch is not so much that they rolled the dice, but rather, that they were willing to accept the results as the answer from God.

The fact that they used this method so frequently says something about their trust in God (unless you just want to chalk it up to a gambling addiction). Either way, that was how they rolled.

How and why those dice landed the way they did would always be unexplainable, yet taken as an acceptably stable answer from the Lord.

I recently heard a dear friend of mine, who also happens to be an elder at a church I oversee in Texas, tell a story from the pulpit about his military career.[14] This particular incident was one of those unexplainable things that caught his attention and eventually turned him towards God.

My friend Tom had grown up around church, but had always resisted making any kind of formal decision to trust Christ. He was a fighter pilot of a C-130 during the Vietnam conflict.

Flying over "the trail" one night on a mission, his plane was locked-on by radar from an enemy ground troops. A SAM missile had been launched and was headed to destroy him and his flight crew.

When he heard the alarm in the cockpit, Tom remembers, "It was surreal, but in an instant, I knew we were all going to die." He made all the evasive moves he was trained to perform, but the missile was still locked on. Suddenly, his radar went blank and they lost contact with the missile.

He said, "There was a lot of shouting on the radio. We were all trying to find that missile!" Suddenly, there was a huge explosion on the ground underneath their plane. There had been some strange malfunction with that particular missile and it fell to the earth and detonated with a large blast.

My friend and his crew were unharmed and spared for some unknown reason. It wasn't long afterwards that Tom gave his heart and life to follow the Lord.

The general reports are that there was about 3,032 aircraft destroyed due to hostile activity during the Vietnam War, with at least that many pilots killed in action. Why was my friend spared? Was there some divine roll-of-the-dice, which allowed him to live through what should have been a sudden and fiery death?

I know how impacted I was just hearing his story. This man has been extremely instrumental in how my own life has played out the past 10 years. I know his wife and sons. I know the people who love, appreciate and respect the contributions he has made in his lifetime. Life would have gone on if he had died that night, but very little today would look like it does today.

Things happen all around us that there are no answers for. Why the *"lot"* lands as it does is a mystery to those of us who put our faith in God's involvement in our lives. Sometimes, the best understanding we have is that **HE is God** and we are not. Come on sevens!

In The Pages

Have you ever had an unexplainable near miss in your life? Has that event changed your life, your way, or your heart? How?

Covering Love

March 17
Proverbs 17

"He who covers a transgression seeks love, but he who repeats a matter separates friends." Proverbs 17:9, NKJV

"He who conceals a transgression seeks love, but he who repeats a matter separates intimate friends." Proverbs 17:9, NASB

What a valuable gem this verse is to the Body of Christ! This very morning, I awoke to headlines in the national news about a young man who was arrested for public intoxication and indecency. It is St Patrick's Day, so I figured the guy was just getting an early start.

The problem is that this man's face and name is attached to a movement that has gained quite a bit of national attention lately. His mission is to bring justice to a tyrant that is exploiting children in a third world country! This thing has even caught momentum with our government officials and military!

When I read the headline, my first thought was, *Bloody hell! I hate the damned devil!*

My second thought was, *Wonder who is going to love this guy through this Niagara Falls of shame that is about to hammer down on him?*

The third thought was, *We need to focus on the good here (stopping crimes against children), keep moving forward and not get emotionally hung up and lose momentum because of one person's stumbling. Surely, we can get past this tiny blip on the radar? Right? Surely we can... right?*

Scripture is full of instructions and encouragement to forgive and restore people from their stumbling. When Peter asked the Lord how many times we're supposed to forgive, Jesus' response is pretty cut and dry:

FORGIVENESS IS REQUIRED EVERY SINGLE TIME!

Here, check it out for yourself:

"Then Peter came to him and asked, 'Lord, how often should I forgive someone who sins against me? Seven times?' 'No, not seven times,' Jesus replied, 'but seventy times seven!'" (Matthew 18:21-22, NLT)

"So watch yourselves! If another believer sins, rebuke that person; then if there is repentance, forgive. Even if that person wrongs you seven times a day and each time turns again and asks forgiveness, you must forgive." (Luke 17:3-4, NLT)

The red-letter stuff is serious business, no doubt! But the thing I saw in today's Proverb was the process of love in any legitimate act of restoration.

The Hebrew word for *"conceals"* or *"covers"* means *"to fill up the gaps,"* and by implication, it suggests *"to cover one's shame or nakedness; to hide a person who is overwhelmed or exposed."* I probably don't have to point out the obvious, but I will anyway:

WE CONCEAL THESE TRANSGRESSIONS, WE HIDE THE PEOPLE, WE LOVE THEM FOR THEIR BENEFIT... NOT OUR OWN.

It's not because we are embarrassed or we're trying to deny something. The fact that we are vested in them, regardless of their crap, confirms that we are well aware of their failures.

Giving them the *space, covering, filling the gaps* and protecting their heart as they attempt to rebound from the "bumps in the road" is the same way the Lord has restored all of us. This is totally the love of Jesus!

**People who are hurting because of their own failure
can't be loved any better than this.**

As true as that statement is, Solomon then gives us another thought to consider. The person who is lovingly restored but won't change and returns to their sin, we still have to forgive them, but their cycle of weakness has the potential to separate them from the people who have loved them the most.

This is when we have to trust God and hope that eventually those people will open their eyes and see the gift they have had in your *covering* love.

In The Pages

How comfortable are you with talking about the moral failures of people you know or know of in the public's eye? What emotions surface in you when you get a bad report on someone? What's the hardest walk you've ever made with another person's failure?

Big Ears

March 18
Proverbs 18

"An intelligent mind acquires knowledge, and the ear of the wise seeks knowledge." Proverbs 18:15, RSV

"And the disciples came and said to Him, "Why do You speak to them in parables?" Jesus answered them, "To you it has been granted to know the mysteries of the kingdom of heaven, but to them it has not been granted. For whoever has, to him more shall be given, and he will have an abundance; but whoever does not have, even what he has shall be taken away from him. Therefore I speak to them in parables; because while seeing they do not see, and while hearing they do not hear, nor do they understand. In their case the prophecy of Isaiah is being fulfilled, which says, 'YOU WILL KEEP ON HEARING, BUT WILL NOT UNDERSTAND; YOU WILL KEEP ON SEEING, BUT WILL NOT PERCEIVE; FOR THE HEART OF THIS PEOPLE HAS BECOME DULL, WITH THEIR EARS THEY SCARCELY HEAR, AND THEY HAVE CLOSED THEIR EYES, OTHERWISE THEY WOULD SEE WITH THEIR EYES, HEAR WITH THEIR EARS, AND UNDERSTAND WITH THEIR HEART AND RETURN, AND I WOULD HEAL THEM.' But blessed are your eyes, because they see; and your ears, because they hear. For truly I say to you that many prophets and righteous men desired to see what you see, and did not see it, and to hear what you hear, and did not hear it." Matthew 13:10-17, NASB

Living in spiritual community where discipleship is a way of life is very challenging. I'm fairly convinced that the only way it works properly is by a process modeled by the Lord and the twelve who followed Him.

Jesus went about doing what He did while they watched, listened, learned, gleaned, and then when the dust settled, they would move close and ask questions for clarity. They usually got a direct answer and a lot more than what they anticipated.

These were serious men following a serious man, and we don't know very much about what they did in their free time. Sewing together what we have from the Gospels, it seems it was "all work and no play."

Probably not, but whatever the case, Jesus mentioned many times that it was important for them to see and hear beyond the natural. There was so much more to learn and understand than what they saw with their eyes or heard with their ears. They needed to go deeper.

They desired to gain understanding from this Rabbi who did nothing like the familiar religious establishment. The only way to get the illumination was to ask questions and use their ears to hear what no one else was willing to hear.

To the credit of those 12 guys, they did light the fuse many times and Jesus provided the fireworks in teaching them with concepts they never would have imagined. No one had ever brought such revelation. And it wasn't for their entertainment. It was for their formation, development and growth.

They were the continuation plan. Wisdom says, *"The ear of the wise seeks knowledge."* They sought by asking questions and by staying silent long enough to allow insight to develop in their minds and hearts. Ears to hear what the Spirit was saying.

In The Pages

From whom are you able to ask questions in your development process? Have you stopped asking questions, or are you spending all your time talking about what you currently know? When do we outgrow discipleship?

Drip, Drip, Drip!

March 19
Proverbs 19

"A foolish child is the ruin of his father, and a contentious wife is like a constant dripping. A house and wealth are inherited from parents, but a prudent wife is from the Lord." Proverbs 19: 13-14, NET

"A parent is worn to a frazzle by a stupid child; a nagging spouse is a leaky faucet. House and land are handed down from parents, but a congenial spouse comes straight from God." Proverbs 19:13-14, MSG

My wife is the Nacho Queen! Give her a fresh bag of bite-sized corn chips, can of re-fried frijoles, sour cream, jalapeños and fresh-grated cheese, and then just stay out of her way while she performs the magic (a moment of silence please). Emeril has got nothing on girlfriend!

Same thing with the fresh pimento cheese spread! Oh baby! She's willing to make the stuff, but it's usually my job to prepare the cheese.

So, while grating some sharp cheddar one day (along with my knuckles), I got to thinking about the things that grate on a man or a woman. What is it that reduces us down, strips our marriages, thins our joy, eats and gnaws at our soul?

Without going real deep, I think the things mentioned here by Solomon really mess with us. It is hard for parents to be at peace if their kids are not advancing positively with their lives. I've seen the faces and hearts of men and women who know their kids have veered off into something that is not good for them.

Yes, in our culture, parents tend to be over-protective, but Solomon uses the words *"foolish"* and *"stupid"* in describing a wayward kid who won't communicate with proper respect towards the people back home.

It can be just as damaging to parents when their children won't honor or respect them. Whether they deserve it or not, God still tells us to honor our parents.

This is even more important if our parents are non-spiritual people!

Kids who "wig out" religiously on their parents are not doing the Kingdom any favors. As young men and women, we are called to respect our parents' home, relationships, efforts to provide, and ways of getting through life. We are accountable for our words and actions towards our parents.

Anything less is totally disrespectful.

Having *SOME* "spiritual enlightenment" doesn't permit anyone to lay down protocols in an elder's house, including our parents (spiritual or natural)!

This thing about the *leaky faucet* or the *constant dripping* is another problem that can grate on us. At first glance, we think this only applies to the wife. Not true. Not even close to being true.

I've never known anyone whose nagging generated a proper heart response from the person who is under barrage. Sure, the nagger may get what they want, but usually it's only because someone has relented in an effort to get the nagging to stop!

Whether it's a mom nagging her kids, a wife nagging her husband, a father nagging his kids, or even kids nagging their parents, the end result is deep-seated resentment.

Nagging usually comes out of a wound, offense, or just plain ol' control. No one is having any fun around this kind of strife and personal irritation!

It eats away at our lives and inner peace. Paul wrote, *"Bearing with one another, and forgiving each other, whoever has a complaint against anyone; just as the Lord forgave you, so also should you"* (Colossians 3:13, NASB).

Surely, we can do better with these matters.

In The Pages

Read it again today: 1 Corinthians 13. Try it in a couple of different translations and compile thoughts that the Spirit may be speaking to you.

Cheap Talk

March 20
Proverbs 20

"Many a man proclaims his own loyalty, but who can find a trustworthy man?" Proverbs 20:6, NASB

So when you give to the poor, do not sound a trumpet before you, as the hypocrites do in the synagogues and in the streets, so that they may be honored by men. Truly I say to you, they have their reward in full. But when you give to the poor, do not let your left hand know what your right hand is doing, so that your giving will be in secret; and your Father who sees what is done in secret will reward you. When you pray, you are not to be like the hypocrites; for they love to stand and pray in the synagogues and on the street corners so that they may be seen by men. Truly I say to you, they have their reward in full. Matthew 6:2-5, NASB

There is a wide variance of translations of today's focus verse. I picked the NASB because I liked the trail the concordance led me down.

The word for *"proclaim"* is **qârâ'** (pronounced *kaw-raw'*), and it means to *"aggressively accost another person with a call or cry."* It forces a decision now, instead of letting people see for themselves over time.

Wisdom suggests that our character declarations might not be totally trustworthy. It's possible that we're hiding something or working much too hard to impress others. It happens all the time. Obviously, God cares about the internal realities and is not impressed with our external charades.

Today's Matthew passage is a prime example of what I'm referring to: *"Do not sound a trumpet before you"* (V:2). I always thought that meant to call attention to yourself by blowing a horn or trumpet. The overall idea is right, but when Jesus spoke these words, he was addressing the Pharisees about their need to be affirmed in their own piety before God.

They were much too smart to blow a horn. No, they had a much more subtle way of accosting attention to themselves when they needed to be affirmed in all of their pageantry.

In the Temple, the box designated to hold and receive the monetary gifts to the Lord had a very large brass funnel (the trumpet) on top of the treasure box. Instead of putting your coins in a tiny slot, you could just set the coin inside the funnel and it would drop easily into the treasure box.

The Pharisees had a nasty habit of holding and releasing their coins up high above the trumpet. Inside those spacious halls, the coins would hit the brass trumpet and make a very loud noise, which echoed all throughout the Temple. Everyone's head would turn, giving the Pharisee what they wanted in the first place:

ATTENTION and the APPLAUSE OF MAN.

Jesus reminds us that God knows the real deal here. *Proclaiming* our love, loyalty or commitment only goes so far. We have to follow these proclamations up with our actions.

Words are not enough.

Wisdom says, "talk is cheap," and it's the heart that really matters.

In The Pages

What was the ugly word that Jesus used for people who liked man's attention regarding their religious activity (Matt 6:5)? What was the real problem with the Pharisees' prayer life? How much of your spiritual activity is purposefully on display before man? How healthy is the Bride of Christ with this topic?

Nickel's Worth of Patience

March 21
Proverbs 21

"The plans of the diligent lead surely to advantage, but everyone who is hasty comes surely to poverty." Proverbs 21:5, NASB

"Do not be hasty in word or impulsive in thought to bring up a matter in the presence of God. For God is in heaven and you are on the earth; therefore let your words be few." Ecclesiastes 5:2, NASB

When I was in fifth grade, I was a great fan of comic books. Archie was a big one for me, and I loved the Fantastic Four and Mad Magazine.

In one of those quality publications, I read and responded to an advertisement where you could purchase 12 vinyl records for a nickel. Such a deal! How could I not partake?

The Rolling Stones, Led Zeppelin, The Moody Blues, Santana, The Fifth Dimension, Steppenwolf, Iron Butterfly, The Doors, Deep Purple, The Beatles and CSNY, just to name the majors.

The package finally arrived and I tore into it like it was Christmas morning. The new tunes, rock-n-roll, electric sex, and great anthems of the '60s and '70s filled the house!

My parents knew exactly what I had done, but waited until the first monthly shipment showed up to have a conversation. Dad brought home that first album, along with a bill for that first monthly installment. I remember specifically asking him, *"What is this?"* I didn't have a clue!

In my great haste to have what I wanted, I had failed to read the small (microscopic) print. That single nickel had dragged me into a contract that authorized the record company to ship me a record (of their choice) every month, for one year.

The price of the record was always inflated and rarely featured tunes played by local radio stations. It was torturous to do chores knowing that my hard earned money was going to pay for stuff I really didn't want. That was one expensive nickel!

"Hasty" is the optimal word here. The two different usages are directly correlated in today's text.

In the Proverbs reference, **ûwts** (pronounced *oots*) means, *"to press or lean in with pressure."* The Ecclesiastes passage uses the word **mâhar** (pronounced *maw-har'*), which denotes *"moving quickly out of an emotional response like fear, anxiety, impatience or heated judgment."*

Either way, it's clear that our impulsive responses are saying something to us about our internal spiritual climate. **Rejection** tells us, *"You'd better grab all you can, while you can, because you'll never get another opportunity to get what you want!"* It totally discounts our trust that our Lord really does love us and does want to give us good gifts (Matthew 7:11). Which means...

We don't have to be impulsive or compulsive.

Debt can, at times, be necessary and legit. But those who are in deep credit card debt (been there), got there usually because they decided to satisfy some internal craving or compulsive desire to have what they can probably do without.

As I said, medical emergencies and other exceptions happen, but that's not the general rule. The stats are heavy in the other direction.

Some of our troubles happen because we don't process our major decisions with the Lord or we get in a hurry. Knowing God's timing is a part of hearing God. We usually get in trouble when we get hasty and move out of compulsive impatience.

In The Pages

One of the fruits of the Spirit is *patience* (Galatians 5:22). Check out the following verses and see how well you are displaying this fruit: Ephesians 4:2; 1 Corinthians 13:4; Colossians 1:11, 3:12; 1 Thessalonians 5:14; 2 Peter 3:9. What are some great qualities of patience?

High Heels

March 22
Proverbs 22

"The reward of humility and the fear of the Lord are riches, honor and life."
Proverbs 22:4, NASB

"Respecting the Lord and not being proud will bring you wealth, honor, and life." Proverbs 22:4, MSG

The NET Bible offers a very interesting insight to the word translated as "reward": *"The Hebrew term **êqeb**, ay'-keb is related to the term meaning, "heel"; it refers to the consequences or the rewards (compensation) that follows (akin to the English expression **"on the heels of"**)".*

Today, the "rewards" listed are *"riches, honor, and life"*. *"Riches"* meaning, *"wealth"* (money and stuff); *"honor"* suggesting *"weight and influence,"* and *"life",* as in, being a life source—"the ability to revive and give life." Those things come **on the heels of** what? That is the big question and the point of the verse.

Before we get to that, I want to mention that **"on the heels of"** surfaces all the time in spiritual formation. Whether we're talking about sowing and reaping, vapor trails, wakes and ripples, or trickle-down, it all points to the fact that we have opportunities to change or influence life dynamics by our choices.

Will the **"on the heels of"** be positive, or will it be negative?

I can't tell you what the *riches* might look like, nor the *honor* or *life*. It's not my job to tell you how that might manifest. My job is to confirm to you that these are very real spiritual dynamics and they are in operation whether you realize it or not.

You can't scream "freeze" into life's big game of "tag" so you can sort out and calculate how well you are doing. You need to decide some things before you go out today, or tomorrow, or the next day. We need to realize that we will reap what we sow.

We are setting "end results" of tomorrow into motion today.

So, if I live angry, I can expect some anger in return. If I live scarce, I can expect scarcity. If I live as a loving person, I should be able to see and receive more love. If I'm not living out of the fruit of the Spirit (via the Spirit's influence), then I should anticipate—and not be too surprised by—the kind of fruit that ends up in my harvest.

You wouldn't plant corn seed in your soil and expect to harvest watermelons next summer, would you?

Back to the question: *What* generates *riches, honor and life?* Wisdom specifically points two things out:

(1) HUMILITY and (2) THE FEAR OF THE LORD.

What's tricky about these two things is that they can be externally demonstrated, but not actually be real internally. We can fool ourselves into thinking that our behavior fulfills these requirements.

Intellectual or external pretense won't suffice either, nor will they produce the rewards that Wisdom is promising. These are actions and ways of living that surface out of character and a transformed heart.

If *humility* and *the fear of the Lord* don't come from out of those places (character and a transformed heart), **it's fraud.**

Most legal contracts that have a promise to pay for services or goods have a clause that negates the entire contract if fraud is involved. Spiritually, that would be the equivalent of religious pretending.

Both of these things—*humility* and *fear of the Lord*—have a real desire to go low, come under, submit to, shelve their agendas, and seek the highest good of what they serve. That is the stuff that generates the rewards that we are all seeking.

In The Pages

Have you ever been with a person who acts humble but you soon realize they are not humble at all? How did you come to that realization? How did it affect you? What kinds of seeds do you want to plant today? Pray and plant! Make it count!

Listen and Heal

March 23
Proverbs 23

"Listen to your father, who gave you life, and do not despise your mother when she is old." Proverbs 23:22, NIV

I was thinking a couple days ago about how many ideas recycle throughout the Proverbs over and over. Like all good attorneys, they keep saying the same things, just in different patterns and sentence structures, until they have us. I like the fact that the repetition gets into us.

Truth and wisdom that we marinate in find their way into the deeper tissues of our lives. Yes, it touches behavior, but we need it to go to the depths. I have really learned to appreciate and to soak in such valued precepts. I sincerely hope you feel the same way!

Our culture laments over sons and daughters who have no connection with their parents. My experience in ministry has taught me that there are more orphans out there than we could ever imagine. Tragedy explains some of it. Neglect brings on most of it. Divorce doesn't help.

I'm still surprised whenever a young adult tells me they've never had real intimate contact with one of their parents. It is much too common and ultimately heartbreaking.

Today's verse brings us back to that Hebrew word **shâma'** (pronounced *shaw-mah'*) once more. One of the literal meanings of *"listen"* is *"to call in an effort to gather."* This pings around in my spirit because I do think this IS something we need to circle the wagons on.

The banner hanging over this verse is *honor*. So I want us to "gather" in response to the call that *honor* is vital for us.

Most likely this instruction to honor our parents is after we are grown. After your 40s, aging is a very interesting season of life. Many senior adults struggle with regrets of how they raised their kids, or they feel like they don't have anything to offer a younger generation. These thoughts are perfectly normal.

Things seem to move much more quickly in social trends. "Old school" senior adults struggle in coping with all the changes. Technological language is foreign, traditional values seem to be evaporating and stuff is just plain different.

Conventional wisdom declares that once our children are grown, it's time to stop injecting parental advice just because we have an opinion. Sagacity suggests that we "older folk" applaud more and command less.

We so desire the best for those behind us, but we also realize that our role is now primarily supportive. That means we have to pack up a warehouse of life experiences and wait until we are asked about some stuff. This is where I think today's text is making a dent in our spirits.

Including your aging parents in the important stuff in your life can be handled in several different ways. One option would be just to keep them informed of things going on in your life. Most parents really do want to know what's up in your world. It blesses them to sniff the air in your swirl.

Another option that gets deeper into *honor* is to ask for their opinions and insights concerning your more complicated mazes. Listening to them doesn't mean you have to be controlled by them.

Your invitation for them to speak into your life is massive!

Besides, you might actually hear some things that help you resolve a few of your issues. It's a win either way!

In The Pages

When is the last time you shared a personal struggle with your parent(s)? What is your greatest concern in doing that? Do you think God knows your concerns about that? What do you need from Him to trust at deeper levels?

Kisses

March 24
Proverbs 24

"He kisses the lips who gives a right answer." Proverbs 24:26, NASB

"Greet one another with a holy kiss. All the churches of Christ greet you." Romans 16:16, NASB

"All the brethren greet you. Greet one another with a holy kiss." 1 Corinthians 16:20, NASB

"Greet one another with a holy kiss." 2 Corinthians 13:12, NASB

"Greet all the brethren with a holy kiss." 1 Thessalonians 5:26, NASB

"Greet one another with a kiss of love. Peace be to you all who are in Christ." 1 Peter 5:14, NASB

The basic premise here is that open honesty and righteous integrity in dialogue are as pleasurable and satisfying as a loving *"kiss on the lips"*. Sincere affection that is willing to display and move with purposeful intent towards "a bond," is compared to straightforward and honest communication among mankind.

This is powerful business, my friends! And don't assume this is automatically true within the Body of Christ. You would think it would be, but it's not.

Most "church" folk, when asked on any given Sunday morning, will give you two thumbs up when asked, *"Sister Evangelist Clarice, how are you doing?"* The standard response is, *"Blessed of God," "Fine," "Great," "Brilliant," "Perfect,"* or a nice combo of any of those chirps listed. That is what they are, "chirps".

These little *"Praise Jesus"* zingers are quite efficient, but misleading and not always exactly truthful. If how things look is what matters, then how things really are never gets dealt with.

Nothing interferes with intimacy like a mask.

If you slept in a different bed than your mate last night because the afternoon fight went unresolved, then you're not *fine*. The *"kiss on the lips"* (i.e. honesty) would be, *"I'm not doing that well. I'm here today because I need God to move on my heart. I'm desperate for His touch on my wounded spirit. I am a mess. Are you willing to pray with me?"*

You won't hear these very often at 10:57 a.m. on Sunday morning. It's bad publicity and *messy* isn't usually welcome in our houses of God.

Really, Judas? That's how you've decided to identify the One you betrayed? That's the signal? That kiss of betrayal, treachery, bribery and death launched the firestorm.

What *they* were going to do had already been decided, but they needed the soldiers to be certain of their target. I can't picture this shameful *kiss* of dishonesty without also picturing these polar opposite kisses mentioned in today's reference verses. We know little of such preference and respect.

I also picture the girl from Luke 7:37-38, a crumpled, snotty mess at Jesus' feet, crying and unable to contain her true feelings any longer. Filled with gratitude for such tangible forgiveness and manifest acceptance, she tenderly kisses His feet.

I have fought back tears multiple times today while these images played through my mind. Such spilled honesty is welcomed in His presence.

In this display of integrity, under the scowl of religious decorum, Jesus defends and receives her transparent *kisses* as a gift unto Himself. *"He kisses the lips"* of those who honestly respond in heart, word and deed.

In The Pages

Why do you think we're not open to share the realness of our lives in the presence of other believers? When is the last time you got real about your own pain or fears around other Christians? Did you get ministry or a pacifying pat on the back?

Black Waters

March 25
Proverbs 25

"What you have seen with your eyes do not bring hastily to court, for what will you do in the end if your neighbor puts you to shame?" Proverbs 25:8, NIV

According to the Bible Knowledge Commentary, *"In Hebrew the words* **seen with your eyes** *are the last words of verse 7 (KJV, NASB). Some versions (NIV, RSV) put those words with verse 8. The phrase makes verse 7 long for a proverb and also makes far less sense there than with verse 8."* (Just a small heads up for the more technically inclined. -MDP-)

Peterson's translation flows beautifully parallel to the overall spirit of the verse, but ignores the instructions about *hastily to court*:

"Don't jump to conclusions—there may be a perfectly good explanation for what you just saw" (Proverbs 25:8, MSG).

Either way, it's clear that Wisdom counsels us to find a way to reconcile our issues without getting tied up in legal proceedings. Solomon said elsewhere, *"The beginning of strife is like letting out water, so abandon the quarrel before it breaks out"* (Proverbs 17:14, NASB).

I can't think of that last verse without remembering a story that my Uncle Joe once told me. South Arkansas is rice country. As a child, it wasn't that uncommon on hot summer days for him to swim, hunt and fish in channels that held river water for flooded rice fields. Electrical gates and timers controlled all water levels in those channels. Good thing Uncle Joe knew those schedules, because being in a channel when the gates opened was dangerous.

One day while seining for frogs in a shallow channel, he wasn't paying attention and the gate opened before he could get out. The water that rushed into that channel where he was playing was filled with cottonmouth snakes and whatever else got sucked through the pipes. The water actually slithered with black reptiles! His only option was to stand still and let the water carry the passengers downstream, sometimes right through his legs.

Nice imagery, I know. But **STRIFE** is like that. There are way too many snakes in that water and "all hell" begs to break loose.

Jesus had some thoughts about litigation:

"Therefore if you are presenting your offering at the altar, and there remember that your brother has something against you, leave your offering there before the altar and go; first be reconciled to your brother, and then come and present your offering. Make friends quickly with your opponent at law while you are with him on the way, so that your opponent may not hand you over to the judge, and the judge to the officer, and you be thrown into prison. Truly I say to you, you will not come out of there until you have paid up the last cent" (Matthew 5:23-26, NASB).

Jesus wasn't laying down new legalism. He was just making an honest appeal to our hearts. *"First be reconciled"* before you worship and *"Make friends quickly"* to resolve the issue before you ever get to court; for when the court decides, it decides legally and someone is going to pay. That someone might be you.

In The Pages

What are good reasons to pursue a legal course of action? Have you ever had to appear in a courtroom? What toll did it take on your spirit man? Is it possible to win a case, but actually lose more than you bargained for? How?

Door Jams and Wrinkled Sheets

March 26
Proverbs 26

"As the door turns on its hinges, so does the sluggard on his bed."
Proverbs 26:14, NASB

I wonder if Solomon had as much fun with this verse as I've had over the years. Today's text might possibly be the Proverb I've quoted the most in the past 25 years—primarily out of good-natured ribbing with Paschall women.

I'm an early riser. Bedtime for me is a real possibility whenever the sun decides to retire for the day. If that is 8:00 pm, so be it! I might be up at 4:00 am, but I love that cycle!

Hot coffee, scripture, journaling, thinking and praying all before dawn! It is my happy time, my quiet time, the time I'm most open to hear what He might have to say. I've been that way a long time.

Now, Patti and the girls are NOT that way! They could easily knock out 10 hours of sleep on a regular basis; on the weekends, the numbers were more like 12 hours. Having to go to work, school or church required everyone to set an alarm clock. But on the days the girls got to sleep in, I'd usually have to peek in to make sure these people were still breathing.

Once my gals had tanked up on their beauty rest, they would make their glorious appearances. With crumpled pajamas, crusty eyes and crazy hair, they'd shuffle over for a hug, or crawl into my lap. This was the moment I would usually greet them with, *"As a door turns on its hinges, so does the sluggard roll over in bed."*

They never smiled... only me. *"Daaaddy!"* As the years passed and the girls got older, they would roll their eyes and ignore me altogether. I guess some people have no appreciation for Solomon's wisdom until after a big bowl of Fruit Loops.

This verse is part of a larger passage about slothfulness (Proverbs 26:13-16). Solomon isn't addressing our legitimate need for rest. He is poking at the *"sluggard"*. And in each of those four verses, he uses that particular word.

The Hebrew word is '**âtsêl** (pronounced *aw-tsale'),* which means (and there is no way to soften this) *lazy, slothful, wants to avoid exertion.* Even though the descriptions of the sluggard in these verses are slightly outrageous, it's no laughing matter when gifted men and women lose motivation and focus.

Whatever it is that derails a person's motivation and drive to move forward, one thing is clear: it's poor stewardship of God-given abilities, gifts and talents.

NO ONE APPRECIATES SLOTHFULNESS. NO ONE!

Hebrews 6 presents a unique challenge that I think applies here. The charge is simple: Don't be lazy with your spirituality!

Meeting Jesus is the best thing that happens to us! But, there is more to Kingdom living than a ride to heaven! There is more than being baptized, going to church and fixating on our doctrine. There is so much more!

Our spiritual fathers and mothers, empowered by the Holy Spirit, planted and prepared a harvest of hope and faith for those who want more!

"And we desire that each one of you show the same diligence so as to realize the full assurance of hope until the end, so that you will not be sluggish, but imitators of those who through faith and patience inherit the promises" (Hebrews 6:11-12, NASB).

But that is going to require the church to get up from its nap.

In The Pages

Are you satisfied with your spiritual expression and experiences? Do you want more? Are you using your spiritual gifts? How free is the Holy Spirit to move in your space?

BFF

March 27
Proverbs 27

"Do not forsake your friend and the friend of your father, and do not go to your brother's house when disaster strikes you—better a neighbor nearby than a brother far away." Proverbs 27:10, NIV

One of the most hurtful things I ever did to myself and to my BFF (Best Friend Forever) happened when I was a senior in high school. We had grown up together. "Inseparable" is about the only word that accurately describes the relationship.

We lived across the street from each other, went to the same church, same schools—pretty much the same everything. Whenever one of us was grounded at home, the other suffered also. It was a genuine "loving brother" relationship. Still is.

In the early '70s, tennis was all the rage again in America. My BFF and I both got swept up in the tide and signed up as "doubles partners" on our school's tennis team.

As sophomores, we were still figuring out the game and didn't fare too well. But by our junior season we had drastically improved, managed to win district and advance to the state playoff system. Our game strengths were totally opposite, so we played well as a team.

Our senior season was earmarked for us to make a dent in the competition and expectations were high for our success. The hours of dedicated practice had honed us into a really good unit. We were stronger, quicker and more agile—poised for some good stuff.

About 3 weeks before the district tournament our part-time tennis coach approached me to suggest I team up with another guy on the tennis team who was a stronger player than both of us. I consulted with no one before agreeing to what she was suggesting. So the switch was made.

When my parents heard about the change, my dad offered truth that my 17-year-old head couldn't yet process *"Son, you are going to regret this decision. We love you. But, you will pay dearly for this one."*

My BFF and his new partner won District that year. My new partner and I lost our very first match at District. It was over. I had lost my stroke, my drive, my confidence... everything! Not to mention almost losing my BFF.

It was a miserable decision and a righteously deserved outcome for my BFF. We did manage to salvage our relationship, which is still in place today, but a less-than-honorable choice by yours truly could have easily flushed the whole deal.

It was a great lesson, but an ugly memory. Thankfully, the banner over my friend's life says: *Loyal, no matter what the cost!* My BFF taught me then. He teaches me still.

In his formative years, David really didn't have too many people who believed in him. In fact, there were only two: Jonathan (BFF) and an old man (Samuel).

Samuel did call him out of obscurity and set him on fire, but his BFF stuck with him through thick and thin (even when Papa Saul was being a nasty booger).

Solomon said elsewhere, *"A man of too many friends comes to ruin, but there is a friend who sticks closer than a brother"* (Proverbs 18:24, NASB). You just know he had heard David honor the loving memory of his BFF!

In The Pages

Read 2 Samuel 9:1. How impacted was David by his relationship with his BFF? How long has it been since you told a close friend what he or she means to you? How can you show your appreciation tangibly?

Off The Grid

March 28
Proverbs 28

"The one who turns away his ear from hearing the law, even his prayer is an abomination." Proverbs 28:9, NASB

"God has no use for the prayers of the people who won't listen to him." Proverbs 28:9, MSG

The older I've gotten, the better I've become with not being able to reconcile everything that happens between man and God. I think I'm actually more comfortable with the mystery of what I can't quite figure out.

I don't pretend to be a theologian or a scholar, but when people scream about "right" doctrine ALL the time, I wonder who gets to determine what is and what is not "right" doctrine? Even if we restricted all truth to only what we read in the Bible, there still seems to be questions that cycle and feed upon themselves to only produce more questions.

Which translation? Whose interpretation? Is there a right way and a wrong way? Is your way the right way, and anyone who disagrees with you is wrong, anti-church, anti-Christ, or preaching "shallow doctrine"?

The Body of Christ doesn't really agree on much. Some pockets of the church agree on some things, and then other pockets do not agree on anything. Even the really big foundation doctrines don't bring overall agreement to the whole church!

A friend of mine used to say:

"The eleven o'clock hour on Sunday morning is the most divided time on the planet—racially, politically, financially, and doctrinally."[15]

We're there, at the church of our choice, for whatever reason we're there, but no one is doing it the same way. Something deep inside my heart tells me that HE is more than ok with some of the diversity.

Honestly, today's verse caught my attention and I've had to think about it quite a bit. I do think Peterson's translation is close enough to what is really being said, but it's still disturbing.

It's probably right, maybe it is, but I can't get too dogmatic in my heart about it.

Does God turn a deaf ear to sinners who don't keep the "old dead rules?" Does God call His children *"abominations"* because we can't agree on how something in the text is supposed to manifest? I'm thankful Jesus never used that word in reference to you or me!

I can work all kinds of scenarios in my mind about the selfish prayer of sinners who need divine help like foxhole religion or something. Yeah, we ask Him for the right lotto numbers and other goofy things, but does our God really have a mute button on his remote?

When we are just plain funky or in need of a good spiritual shower and proper perspective, does the Almighty reject our request for direction? How do we know whether or not the manifest "quiet" of God is because He's upset, ignoring or rejecting us? Honestly, I'm not in deep enough to know these kinds of things!

So, here is where I've set up camp with this verse: I believe that God is not playing games with us. I think He knows our motivations and our desires. He knows the difference between real and religion (although man sure has trouble deciphering between the two).

ANY PRAYER THAT COMES FROM OUR HEART GETS INTO HIS HEART.

Even when I was dead in my sin (rejecting His love by alienating myself with my rebellious ways), He heard me pray, *"Lord, I need you!"* He heard my prayer and He's heard many others!

When I cry in my brokenness, *"I'm guilty,"* forgiveness always comes. If He doesn't hear these kinds of prayers, I'd be off the spiritual grid altogether!

His mercy endures forever!

In The Pages

So what are your thoughts or questions after reading today's text? What points would you use to disagree with me? (*No yelling please. My ears are working just fine!*)

Dominium

March 29
Proverbs 29

"If a ruler listens to falsehood, all his officials will be wicked." Proverbs 29:12, NRSV

"If a ruler hearken to lies, all his servants are wicked." Proverbs 29:12, KJV

I've told you that I have this concern about redundancy, right? As of today (3/29/11), I can look back and see that I've written over 200 devotionals. No, these are not excerpts from my previous writings, because I don't have previous writings or published works. Each one arrives fresh daily and I put on paper what I think He's telling me to write. That's why I can't get too stressed about the redundancy.

I've read and thought about most of these verses many times over the years. What I've consistently discovered is that He has the unfathomable ability to take what's common or familiar, and highlight different elements in order to teach me things that are spot-on and in alignment with my circumstances.

Incredibly, an old truth becomes a new truth that washes over my spirit like a hot shower on a cold winter night. If I allow these kinds of reminders to revisit me, it helps me chill out with the agendas of what I put on paper.

I can trust Him to "tailor" my reflections to what your heart might need to hear. I can even hope these thoughts might help a young pastor or missionary. Not every message a messenger delivers will land on every listening ear the same way.

God can take the simplest things, hidden things, that might even be missed by an entire congregation, and literally blow the mind of just one person who needed that word, in that season, on that day! The prospects of such a transaction are thrilling. My thanks again, for reading and opening your heart to what God is simultaneously doing through all of us. Really... thanks!

Usually, when I'm deciding on the verse I'm going to expand upon, I get a single word about that verse, in my mind's eye. That's my direction, the compass; ultimately, my starting point. Today, the word I got over this verse was "dominion."

The origin of "dominion" is Medieval Latin, *dominio or dominium*, meaning *"lord or master which influences other men."* Noting the influence is sort of the point, I think. No use overstating the obvious, so on to the questions.

What kind of influence are you? Seriously, when you show up, what is the outcome? Is it positive or negative?

Remember the anti-smoking campaign in the late '60s that featured a little boy watching his dad light a cigarette? There were no speaking parts to the commercial, only the imagery. The message was very powerful. Someone is watching and being influenced by you.

Today's text makes that very clear. Do you want your home to be religious or spiritual? Do you desire real intimacy, or the appearance of intimacy with your mate? Do you want to curb complaining, or be the instigator of complaining?

In terms of sin, what are some doors you have opened and exposed others to? When you are afraid, who else feels that fear? Are you desperate enough for the things around you to change, that you're willing to change first?

In The Pages

You've got the questions… take some time to reflect on your answers.

"Wonder" full

March 30
Proverbs 30

"There are three things which are too wonderful for me, four which I do not understand: the way of an eagle in the sky, the way of a serpent on a rock, the way of a ship in the middle of the sea, and the way of a man with a maid. This is the way of an adulterous woman: she eats and wipes her mouth, and says, "I have done no wrong." Proverbs 30:18-20, NASB

There is a subtle brilliance in these reflections by Agur. This sage of wisdom, who appears very humble, believes that God aids and answers those who seek his help (Proverbs 30:1-6). I like the fact that you have to rest in his writings without demanding an obvious lesson from what he is trying to teach. You need the Spirit to speak to you about the "meat" of his thoughts.

Scholarship helps us with insight, but we still have to quiet ourselves in patience. It's like sucking hard candy. It's probably best not to get in a big hurry. Enjoy the reflections, sit in the observations and think about what we rarely consider.

Today's verses are all tied together with the words, *"the way."* He designates that three of these *ways* are wonderful, though four are not *understandable*. The *"eagle in the sky"*, the *"ship on water"*, and the *"serpent on a rock"* are all examples of things that don't leave a trace of their mobility. They are "wonder" full, wondrous, ultimately marvelous.

Next, he brings up the topic of sexual intimacy of covenant lovers, when he gives an example of what is inappropriate, or out-of-sync, with God's good plan for man. Again, the *ways* of love, both tangibly present and externally relevant, are incredibly "wonder" full, but the real substance lays with what is going on internally.

Sure, we can relish in all the physiological and emotional benefits of sex, but words can't begin to describe the mystical joys and spiritual connections of actual *lovemaking*. Yes, we can describe the act with words and symbols, but the spiritual transactions that affect unity, oneness, love and lifelong connectedness, are beyond casual language.

I'm not sure we can ever get to the bottom of these divine triggers in our God-given sexuality. It's all above us. Too much to comprehend! But, we're good with that, right?

The fifth *"way"* again leaves the sage stupefied. *"I have done no wrong."* This leaves the old oracle dumbfounded. How can this be? How can someone get his or herself involved in something so deep spiritually, without realizing the ultimate ramifications of what is happening? Casually, the adulterer *"eats and wipes,"* and proclaims that nothing has happened. You can hear the arguments:

> *"It's just sex... that is what people do." "This is acceptable behavior."*
> *"Men have needs... women have needs." "It's normal and common."*

Yes it is, in this particular context, much too common.

We should desire the *"wonder,"* but all within the safe and permissible boundaries of spiritual covenant. God will give us the mystery of "one flesh" and the joys of exploring the unknowable. The depths of His divine goodness are awesome and "wonder" full indeed!

In The Pages

How often do you sit in the awareness of how wonderful the unknowable things of God are? Do you have a religious or a spiritual answer for everything? Does that question offend you? Why or why not?

Angels Without Wings

March 31
Proverbs 31

"Give beer to those who are perishing, wine to those who are in anguish; let them drink and forget their poverty and remember their misery no more." Proverbs 31:6-7, NIV

"He causes the grass to grow for the cattle, and vegetation for the labor of man, so that he may bring forth food from the earth, and wine which makes man's heart glad, so that he may make his face glisten with oil, and food which sustains man's heart." Psalms 104:14-15, NASB

I'm not sure I know what all churches do with these verses. I actually laughed out loud while digging through my familiar commentaries, noticing the obvious avoidance of the fact that God played a role in man's abilities to make beer and wine.

In the commentary on today's Psalms text, the cattle, vegetation, food, and olives are all mentioned, along with the benefits of each, but not the wine. I guess it's still a touchy subject.

I think the idea that alcohol was to be used only for medicinal purposes is a bit of a stretch, but to each his own. If that is what you want to believe, or that is what your belief system upholds, then fine. If we can all refrain from judgment when it comes to our differing opinions on this taboo subject, we'll all prove we've grown a bit.

Today, I've been thinking about the ministry of Hospice. This ministry is a concept, not a place.

Their unique focus is to help patients and families deal with a terminal illness. The treatment Hospice offers is palliative, not curative. They treat pain and minister comfort. The volunteers are trained to prepare the patient and family for death. They assure the sick that death is as normal as life. It requires an awesome amount of sensitivity because each "passing" is different. They actually facilitate the heart of what today's text is conveying.

A dear friend who works with Hospice told me that she has seen and heard things which have confirmed the spiritual awesomeness of a person's transition from life to life through death. She is absolutely convinced that God is there in the process and that there is a place prepared for us after we take our last breath here on earth (John 14:1-4).

I've heard her make comments like, *"The things patients say and describe in their final moments are eerily common. It seems like they're all describing the same place."* They probably are.

Our hospitals, nursing homes and medical communities are filled with "angels" who minister in amazing grace and loving mercy! The professionals are sharp no doubt, but these volunteers who offer their unique talents of love bring an element of peace and comfort to the patients and their families that is unsurpassed by any standard! Angels without wings is what they are!

When I read today's Proverb, I'm not hearing an excuse for people to go get "wasted" on drugs and alcohol. But I sense the mercy of God. He is the lifter of our heads, the lover and healer of our souls! His patience and tender kindness find us.

In The Pages

Do you know people who volunteer in the medical community? Write out their names and offer a prayer of thanksgiving and blessing over their lives. We need them to do what they do!

ENDNOTES

January 9 - [1]Michael R. Hindes. Quote used by permission. Michael and Kathy Hindes are the founders of Kingdom, Inc. They are pastors, lovers, teachers, encouragers, disciplers, leadership developers, good parents to both natural and spiritual children, servants, and maybe the two people who have believed the most in Patti and I since we've been in ministry. They are the kind of friends you can't categorize. They are more family than friend. We love them dearly. It is an amazing privilege to walk and serve in the Kingdom with these two!

January 16 – [2]Andrew Shearman, a longtime friend in the ministry. Quote used by permission. Andrew was there for Patti and I as we plowed in brutally hard soil at times. He's always been a sound voice of encouragement and hope. Andrew (and his wife Mo) is the founder of the G42 Leadership Academy located in Mijas Pueblo, Spain. I still contend he's the prettiest man in Europe.

January 21 – [3]Peter Lord was Pastor of Park Avenue Baptist Church in Titusville, FL for over 30 years. Peter is a gifted author and popular conference speaker. Peter and his wife Johnny really ministered to Patti and I as we made our transition out of denominational life back in the early '90's http://peterlord.net; [4]President Franklin D. Roosevelt. Quote from his first inaugural address (1933).

January 27 – [5]Richard Rohr. *Adam's Return: The Five Promises of Male Initiation*. Published by the Crossroad Publishing Company. Richard uses this quote in many of his writings and sermons. Father Richard has mentored me through his writings and tapes since 2005. I've never met him. I hope to one day!

February 8 – [6]*On Pilgrimage With Father Richard Rohr* (1983—4 tapes). St. Anthony Messenger Press.

February 12 – [7]Michael R. Hindes sermon notes. Used with the permission of Dr. Bob Nichols.

February 16 – [8]Jonathan and Melissa Helser are extremely anointed worship people. Their albums are fresh and alive with all kinds of creative flavors of the Spirit. They also host and lead an incredible ministry called 18 Inch Journey at their farm in Sophia, NC. If I were 21 again, there would be little doubt; I'd be all IN! We love them so much! Check'em out: http://jonathanhelser.com

February 24 – [9]Olan Miles started the Texas Baptist Men Retiree Builders back around 1975. He was probably pushing 80 when I met him in 1987. I loved that old man! He was something else.

February 26 – [10]Dave and Sara Barteaux have served many years as Southern Baptist missionaries in the Middle East. They are dear friends and quite the inspiration and example for all of us. Finer people you'll never meet!

February 29 - [11]Evely, Louis, translated by Bonin, Edmond. *That Man Is You.* Copyright © The Missionary Society of St. Paul The Apostle in the State of New York, USA.

March 4 – [12]I met Cody Hodges through my kids. Cody graduated from Texas Tech University in 2005. I invite you to Google his numbers. This dude could really throw a football. He's a good man. A keeper.

March 11 - [13]David Johnson is not only one of my best friends, but one of the finest bible teachers I've ever known. He is the Sr. Pastor of Church of the Open Door, Maple Grove, MN. He and his precious wife Bonnie have 4 kids and 6 grandchildren.

March 16 – [14]Thomas McPherson serves as an Elder at Emmanuel Christian Fellowship in McGregor, Texas. He and his wife are great friends to Patti and I. We love them dearly.

March 28 – [15]Ronald Peacock and his wife Linda began to show Patti and I the spiritual ropes of Spirit-filled living soon after we left the SBC. Few men are more anointed than the "Goat Farmer Prophet." He's a modern-day wild-man, but a lover to the core! He's showed me how joy and brokenness work together.

RESOURCES

BIBLE KEY:

KJV - *The Holy Bible, King James Version* (Public Domain).

MSG – Peterson, E. H. (2005). *The Message: the Bible in contemporary language*. Colorado Springs, CO: NavPress. Used by permission.

NASB - *New American Standard Bible: 1995 update*. (1995). LaHabra, CA: The Lockman Foundation. Used by permission.

LXX - Brenton, L. C. L. (1870). *The Septuagint Version of the Old Testament: English Translation*. London: Samuel Bagster and Sons.

NCV - *The Everyday Bible: New Century Version*. (2005). Nashville, TN: Thomas Nelson, Inc. Used by permission.

NET - Biblical Studies Press. (2006). *The NET Bible First Edition; Bible. English. NET Bible.; The NET Bible*. Biblical Studies Press. Used by permission.

NIV – *THE HOLY BIBLE, NEW INTERNATIONAL VERSION®*. Copyright © 1973, 1978, 1984 by International Bible Society. Used by permission.

NKJV - *The New King James Version*. (1982). Nashville: Thomas Nelson. Used by permission.

NLT - *New Living Translation* (1996, 2005, 2007). Tyndale House Publishers, Inc., Carol Stream, Illinois 60188. Used by permission.

NRSV - *The Holy Bible: New Revised Standard Version*. (1989). Nashville: Thomas Nelson Publishers. Used by permission.

RSV - *Revised Standard Version of the Bible*, copyright 1952 [2nd edition, 1971] by the Division of Christian Education of the National Council of the Churches of Christ in the United States of America. Used by permission.

TLB – *The Living Bible* (1971) Tyndale House Publishers, Inc., Wheaton, IL 60189. Used by permission.

YLT - *The Young's Literal Translation Bible* (Public Domain).

OTHER HELPS:

Baxter, J. Sidlow (1960). *Awake My Heart*. Copyright © 1960. Zondervan Publishing Company, Grand Rapids, MI.

Blue, J. R. (1985). James. (J. F. Walvoord & R. B. Zuck, Eds.)*The Bible Knowledge Commentary: An Exposition of the Scriptures*. Wheaton, IL: Victor Books.

Chambers, Oswald (1935). Original edition © 1935. *My Utmost For His Highest*. Dodd, Mead & Company, Inc., New York, NY.

Jamieson, R., Fausset, A. R., & Brown, D. (1871). *Commentary Critical and Explanatory on the Whole Bible*. (Public Domain).

Keil, C. F., & Delitzsch, F. (1996). *Commentary on the Old Testament*. Peabody, MA: Hendrickson.

Peterson, Eugene H. (2007). *Conversations: THE MESSAGE with It's Translator*. Copyright © 2007 by Eugene H. Peterson. All rights reserved. THE MESSAGE Numbered Edition copyright © 2005. NavPress Publishing Group, Colorado Springs, CO.

Rohr, Richard. *Adam's Return: The Five Promises of Male Initiation*. Copyright © 2004. Crossroad Publishing Company, New York, NY. Used with permission.

Rohr, Richard. Preparing for Christmas: Daily Meditations for Advent. Copyright © 2008. Franciscan Media, Cincinnati, OH. Used with permission.

Rohr, Richard and Feister, John. *Radical Grace: Daily Meditations by Richard Rohr*. Copyright © 1995. St. Anthony Messengers Press, Cincinnati, OH. Used with permission.

Ryrie, Charles Caldwell (1995). *The Ryrie Study Bible, New American Standard*: with introductions, annotations, outlines, marginal references, harmony of the Gospels, synopsis of Bible doctrine, index of Scripture, index to notes, concordance, maps, and timeline charts, and many other helps. Expanded edition. Scripture taken from the NEW AMERICAN STANDARD BIBLE®, Copyright© 1960, 1962, 1963, 1968, 1971, 1972, 1973, 1975, 1994 by the Lockman Foundation. Used by permission.

Strong, J. (2009). *A Concise Dictionary of the Words in the Greek Testament and The Hebrew Bible*. Bellingham, WA: Logos Bible Software.

Thomas, R. L. (1998). *New American Standard Hebrew-Aramaic and Greek dictionaries : updated edition*. Anaheim: Foundation Publications, Inc.

Thomas, R. L., The Lockman Foundation. (1998). *New American Standard exhaustive concordance of the Bible: updated edition*. Anaheim: Foundation Publications, Inc.

ACKNOWLDEGEMENTS

I would be remiss if I didn't thank some people. Patti Paschall, the love of my life, is the one who prodded me the most to start putting my thoughts on paper. For over 35 years, she's been the one to lead the charge to encourage me. No one has believed in me more. Her "I love this" has been quite the life source. She is my Jesus with skin. She has everything to do with my finishing this project. I can't imagine such a venture without her being beside me. My one, my only, my queen. xo

My children and grandchildren also provide the most amazing motivation to spill the goods. My girls and their guys are spiritually very serious and engaged. They're on the edge, and they push me to peak over their ledge from time to time. I love their views. Nicole, Steve, Paige, and Jon: I could not be more blessed by you. xo

One thought that really helped me chill out and be real was the idea that one day my grandbabies will be Kingdom fire-breathers. They'll be much more aggressive in the Spirit than myself, but maybe there is enough here to feed them for a season or two. Isabel Rose, Jones Michael, Lewis Christian, Grace Irene, and those to follow: you are perfection in my heart! xo

I wrote and compiled the first month of devos in January 2010 and presented them to 18 of my intimate peers. I asked them for honest feedback. A few did indeed respond, but the majority never said a word. To those few who did respond, I got some major encouragement. Thank you.

In fact, it was my son-in-law, Jon, who drove the decisive nail when he asked me, *"Ba, who is your audience?"* Baaamm! I knew this project wasn't necessarily going to be for "church people." Anyone was welcome to read it, and I was totally fine with that, but the people Patti and I were mentoring as we traveled the globe were the audience that pulled on my heart. I wanted to talk to young men and women who were not hung up in some sort of religious system. From that point on, it was game on. Whether or not I accomplished that with this devo is yet to be seen.

I had a group of people I called the "Devo Club," who read the stuff I was emailing them weekly. Their faces were the ones I pictured when I was writing. Some of them periodically commented and offered suggestions. All of them encouraged me to keep going forward. Taryn Mast, Rocio Doyle, Darci Simpson, Jennifer Goeddertz, Megan Dietrich, Sara Hansen, Dennis Gable, Sarah Lapp Clements, Ashley Higgins, Erika Baldwin, and Kellen Gorbett. Thanks guys! I love you people dearly!

But there were two other members of the Devo Club who gave me feedback on a daily basis. Kayla and Andrea journaled their responses to each day's lesson and basically allowed me to peek into their hearts as they were processing the material. I can't even begin to explain how that kept me going!

Kayla Phillips Hindes was the voice of an angel. She reeks of encouragement anyway, but she really honed her craft when I needed it the most! Thanks baby. I'll owe you forever.

Andrea Gosselin jumped in during the editing process. She made her deeply vulnerable thoughts available to me on a daily basis. What a gift you are, woman! I love what you have with the Lord!

I have had two editors with this project, Erika and David. Erika Baldwin is a true spiritual daughter, but also an amazing wife to Bradley and a committed mother to Hannah and Luke. What it cost her to edit this project is a debt I'll never be able to repay. The Lord spoke clearly to me that she was to be my editor long before I asked her. Patti and I prayed hard about it. We knew this would be a drain on her family. Erika and I were in constant communication throughout the process—a time I'll always cherish. She was perfect for me. She clarified my scribbling without me having to lose my voice. That was what I wanted. That is what I got. Thanks babe! Love you! xo

David Reyes is a busy man. Too busy actually, but he volunteered to be the final eyes before we published ***RAW TALKS WITH WISDOM – Not Your Grandma's Devo***. His gorgeous wife Catherine (now carrying twins) and precious daughter Liv have patiently shared their David throughout this effort. David is a good son. He's served when he really didn't have the time or energy to do it. I'm grateful for his love and devotion. Thanks dude! xo

Once we decided to test readership with an email version of ***RAW TALKS WITH WISDOM – Not Your Grandma's Devo***, it simply would not have happened without Allison Johnston. She basically said, "I'll handle it," and that is exactly what she did. Allison would disappear for a week and then show up and say, "Look at this!" It was awesome! She also took all the pictures we used in the email version. She is the epitome of a spiritual daughter. Perfection really. Love you so much. xo

Jon Egan (my son by marriage) massaged the pics to make the images what we needed them to be. He's the one that has produced most of the graphics and set the overall ambience for the project. He also designed the cover and the Title Page. Again, he just fixed stuff. He always does. What a gift you are to God's people and to me. xo

And then there are the thousands of people who have allowed Patti and I to speak into their lives. I know what I know, and have learned what I have learned, because people were willing to ask me what I thought, and then give me space in their lives to work it out with them.

As I spoke, ministered, discipled, pastored, mentored, and tried to love, I learned a lot about people and probably even more about myself. Even when the stuff coming out of my mouth wasn't too good, most have loved on me well throughout the seasons. I do not deserve all the ways in which I have been honored. Not in the least. Thank you for your trust. I love you all.

And Lord, thank you for your patience, mercy, and unfailing love. You've changed me... from the inside out.

Thank you for everything! I am a blessed man!

Mike
2013

AUTHOR

Mike Paschall was born in Pine Bluff, Arkansas, but raised in Texas. He is a graduate of the University of Arkansas-Fayetteville with a BSEd. He also graduated from Southwestern Baptist Theological Seminary in Ft. Worth, Texas with an MDiv. Mike has served as pastor at numerous churches since 1987 and currently serves as pastor in the United Methodist Church. Mike and Patti were married in 1977. They have two daughters (Nicole, married to Steven Brewer, and Paige, married to Jon Egan) and six grandchildren (Isabel Rose, Jones Michael, Lewis Christian, Grace Irene, Esther Jane, and William Michael) who all live in Colorado Springs, CO. Mike loves any opportunity to mentor young pastors, missionaries, men and women who are passionate about ministry and Kingdom. He also loves preaching, teaching, and writing about the things of God. He is also particularly fond of a good hang with family, a cigar with a great friend, his Indian motorcycle, and an occasional trip to the golf course.

"David once told his son, Solomon, "Wisdom is the principle thing." I think every son craves a father that knows and lives that truth. Mike has taken me (and so many others) under his wing as a son and daily allowed me to grow by experiencing his wisdom, which was earned through all types of joys and sorrows. Wisdom IS the principle thing, and Mike models that by the way he lives, leads, shares and writes!" David Brown - Minister to Youth, Bella Vista Baptist Church, Bella Vista, AR.

"This devo is made most powerful by the man that lives the words every day. Mike Paschall's insights are a testament to a life worth the journey. More than a collection of daily readings—but a lifetime of wisdom, love, and challenge poured onto these pages. RAW TALKS WITH WISDOM will provoke you, inspire you, and make you scratch your head a bit. Often challenging the status quo that was lodged in my spirit, this devo led me to examine fully, wonder longer, and love deeper." Allison Johnston - COO at Umba "an e-commerce platform for handmade goods," Atlanta, GA.

"Paschall is one of my best friends. Actually more than that, he's my priest. It's usually to him I go when I need a safe place to land my failures. I normally find brutal truth dripping with amazing grace. Regarding this book, it's become one my favorite daily meditations. Mike writes like he lives - vulnerable, honest, and real. WARNING, this book isn't for the staunchly, overly religious, or spiritual know-it-alls. It's a devotional for regular folks, just like us..." Michael Hindes - coach, teacher, father, President of Kingdom Inc., Atlanta, GA.

"Real, Raw, Biblical, Wise - did I say Raw? Yep - a lot like Mike, is this daily devo he's written, and it's what I love about it (and him). I've known Mike for over 25 years, and one of the things you can count in from him is that he'll tell it to ya straight - no song and dance - no shifting shadows - no wondering "what did he mean by that?" What's best, however, is that his straight talk comes from a place of wisdom, knowledge, experience, and love. There are few people in the planet whose opinion I value more, so just subscribe to the damn devo and read it! Good stuff!" David Johnson – Sr. Pastor at Church of the Open Door, author of *The Subtle Power of Spiritual Abuse*, Maple Grove, MN.

"Mike Paschall is my friend... this Devo is a frank, edgy communication of truths from the heart of God. I love Mike because of his honesty and transparency. If Jesus were talking to his disciples, or to the people of the day, I think he would smile at the conversational communications of this son. If you want a normal religious devotional reading, there are many available... but for those that have embarked on an honest difficult journey with a living Christ... I recommend Mike's Devo's... they will leave you thinking, crying, laughing and challenged." Dr. Bob Nichols - pastoral coach, counselor, teacher, Bellingham, WA

"Mike Paschall's mental and spiritual meanderings are thought provoking and interesting. Mike, who pastored mainstream churches in the past, presents a first hand account of religion, as some of us knew it, with a modern dose of common sense and the realization that all things change and deserve a re-look. Agree with Mike or not you will never be bored and his thoughts will cause you to think. Today's Christianity is due a new look and Christians owe it to themselves and others to use the critical thinking skills God gave us all." Rev. Paula Brown - A true West Texas girl, political purveyor, and forever poster-child of the 60's, Moody, TX.

"If it is real bread from God you want you have picked up the right book. Mike is a very real minister of the gospel that knows what you need when you wake up and you are starving for God to give you a Word for your life. Mike will blast you in the heart with his unique gifted use of language. Mike is one of the most important friends I have in the world. I have known Mike for over twenty-five years as one of my accountability friends. When I need a word from God, in a language that can only come from the Holy Spirit, I call Mike. He is truly gifted with speaking a tongue that you will understand. His devotional guides will guide you to the throne of God." Bart McMillan – Business Chaplain, President of Life's Lesson's Ministries, Gainesville, GA.

"As someone who has rarely done daily devotions, I did not know if I would keep up or stick with it. I've done both, and have thoroughly enjoyed and benefited from these daily "nuggets" of wisdom. These writings are insightful and thought provoking. I look forward to my devotion time every day." David Taylor - Senior

Academic Consultant at a large private university, married father-of-two, McGregor, TX.

"Mike's devotionals are open, honest and refreshing. But most of all they are unfiltered by the spirit of "religion" that has invaded so much of biblical teaching in the world today. His desire for us to know the real Jesus is apparent in all that is included in this work. Whether you are a committed follower of Jesus Christ or seeking in your spiritual journey, I recommend this book for you." Barry Strickland - Texas Director of New Wilderness Adventures, Lancaster, TX.

"One of the characteristics of Mike Paschall that I greatly respect is his direct approach. He has a gift for unpacking principles and truths from God's Word and putting them in down-to-earth and in-your-face words that make it impossible to wiggle away from their weightiness. In RAW TALKS WITH WISDOM, Mike shares a daily dose of truth, without the sugar coating, that will lead you to a deeper relationship with God." Stephanie Pridgen - Missionary Church Administrator for International Christian Assembly, Kiev, Ukraine.

"Nothing strikes of more importance to me than 'a real Christian' and by that I mean a raw, lay it out on the table, I've made mistakes, and this is who I am Christian. We are called to make disciples and I truly believe we can't do that until we are real with each other. And that is why RAW TALKS WITH WISDOM is truly amazing. They are as real and raw as it gets. I truly believe the "church" is afraid to talk that way, but through Mike and his devos I have been able to face obstacles that I can assure you are not pretty or clean, but that is life and thank God somebody like Mike is not afraid to speak right to the heart of what life is really all about!" Taryn Mast – Performance Coach, San Diego, CA.

"To know Mike is to love him dearly or not at all, mostly because he leaves very little margin for misunderstanding. RAW TALKS WITH WISDOM is beautiful for that very reason; it is a heartfelt journey through the book of Proverbs that will lead you gracefully into a deeper relationship with Wisdom. 'In The Pages' offers an opportunity for each reader to work through the details as their story collides with God's story through the scriptures. If you are looking for a devotional that will make you feel safe, this isn't it. If you're searching for a daily opportunity to be honest with yourself and with God, then dive in... just keep in mind, this isn't your grandma's devo!" Dennis Gable – A multi-faceted, uniquely gifted Kingdom communicator who lives with his gorgeous wife and beautiful children in Phoenix, AZ.

www.ingramcontent.com/pod-product-compliance
Lightning Source LLC
Chambersburg PA
CBHW021951290426
44108CB00012B/1020